Collected Lyrics

1970 – 2015

PATTI SMITH

An Imprint of HarperCollins*Publishers*

HarperCollins books may be purchased for educational, business, or sales promotional use. For information please e-mail the Special Markets Department at SPsales@harpercollins.com.

This is a revised, updated, and expanded edition of a book first published in 1988 by Doubleday, a division of Bantam Doubleday Dell Publishing Group, Inc.

Designed by Suet Yee Chong

Library of Congress Cataloging-in-Publication Data has been applied for.

ISBN 978-0-06-234501-1

15 16 17 18 19   OV/RRD   10 9 8 7 6 5 4 3 2 1

In memory of Fred Sonic Smith,
1948–1994

The typewriter is holy the poem is holy the voice is holy the hearers are holy the ecstasy is holy!

—ALLEN GINSBERG,
"FOOTNOTE TO HOWL"

COLLECTED LYRICS

To Find a Voice

We all have a song.

A song comes spontaneously, expressing joy, loneliness, to dispel fear or exhibit a small triumph. We hardly notice we are forming them, as we sing them, often alone, half to ourselves.

It is finding the words within that leads us to sing. It might be a hymn, a shard of rebellion, or a teenage prayer. We discover inspiration where we may, in an old guitar in the corner of a garage, under a bed, or hanging in a pawnshop window. In a phrase carried to us by the wind, walking along. In the reflection we see of ourselves in the mirror. Sometimes we recognize our song in the song of another. It is the miracle of the popular song, songs that are beloved universally, often in their simplicity.

The evolution of such little songs into poetry, improvisational performance and collaboration produced these lyrics, written with great hopes to strike some chord, reaching a listener who finds their meaning within, and sings along.

The first song I remember singing is "Jesus Loves Me." I can picture myself singing it while sitting on a stoop in Chicago, waiting for the organ grinder to come up the street with his pet monkey. I can hear the songs that were in the air. "Day-O" and "Shrimp Boats" and "Heart of My Hearts." I can hear my father whistling "Deep Purple" and the voice of my mother as she sang us to sleep.

I recall my first record player, only slightly larger than a lunchbox, and my two records, one red and one yellow: "Tuby the Tuba" and "Big Rock Candy Mountain." I loved watching them spin, contemplating the worlds they evoked. But the song that produced my first visceral reaction was sung by Little Richard.

It was Sunday. My mother and I hand in hand. She was taking me to Bible school. She had kid gloves on like the White Rabbit in *Alice in Wonderland*. They gave her a special air and I admired them tremendously. We passed the boys' clubhouse—two huge refrigerator boxes cut and pieced together. Ritchie Glasgow was spinning sides and what wafted from the hand-cut window (more for breathing than for seeing) stopped me dead in my tracks, causing me to let go of my mother's hand so abruptly as to remove her glove.

I didn't know what I was hearing or why I reacted so strongly. It wasn't "Shrimp Boats" or "Day-O." It was something new, and though I didn't comprehend what drew me, drawn I was. Drawn into a child's excited dance. That was "Tutti Frutti," so alien, so familiar. That was Little Richard. That was for me the birth of rock and roll.

For a time we lived in Philadelphia. Everyone liked to sing and dance. My sister and I would jitterbug. People sang a cappella on the street corners. When I was nine, we moved to South Jersey. My music teacher adored opera. He would bring his albums to class and play us selections from Verdi and Puccini. I was taken with this music and I was especially moved by Maria Callas. Her emotional intensity. How she seemed to draw from every fiber to create a whisper. Her arias soared from the turntable—especially my favorite, the opera hit single "Un bel dì." For a time I dreamed of being an opera singer, but I didn't have the calling, the discipline, or the necessary physical frame. My teacher, sensing my desire, gave me a glorious task. As Manrico I sang the lullaby from Verdi's *Il Trovatore*. For a brief moment I was able to feel the troubadour's expansive love for his home in the mountains.

I dreamed of being a jazz singer like June Christie and Chris Connor. Of approaching songs with the lethargic charge of Billie Holiday. Of championing the downtrodden like Lotte Lenya's "Pirate Jenny." But I never dreamed of singing in a rock and roll band. They had yet to exist in my world. But my world was rapidly changing.

I was privileged to evolve during an inspired period of spiritual and cultural revolution. And the music was the revolution where all had a voice and through this voice we united. Our battlefields were Ohio, Chicago, the Fillmore. We gave new meaning to the word "soldier." We were slinging an electric guitar instead of a machine gun.

I broke from the confines of a rural existence. Farewell the factory, square-dance hall, the withering orchards. I headed for New York City. I had in mind to become a painter and through that pursuit I found my beat and the root of my voice. Standing before large sheets of paper tacked to a wall, frustrated with the image I'd draw words instead— rhythms that ran off the page onto the plaster. Writing lyrics evolved from the physical act of drawing words. Later, refining this process led to performance.

In 1969 I moved to the Chelsea Hotel with Robert Mapplethorpe. By then I had abandoned hope of becoming a painter. I was offered work in underground theater. It was too confining. I longed to spar with the people, to make contact. Robert encouraged me to perform my poetry. I attended readings but found them even more confining than theater. Bob Neuwirth suggested I put my lyric style to music and Sam Shepard used two pieces in his play *Mad Dog Blues.*

On February 10, 1971, I gave my first poetry reading, opening for Gerard Malanga at St. Mark's Church on the Bowery. In desiring to project a raw energy, I recruited Lenny Kaye. We climaxed the reading with his sonic interpretation of a stock car race with electric guitar while I read "Ballad of a Bad Boy." It seemed to have a negative effect. I took that as a positive sign.

In the next few years I took to studying Hank Williams, got me a Bob Dylan songbook, banged away on an old thirties Gibson. I worked in a bookstore. I drew. I modeled for Robert. Scrawled in my notebooks. I wandered through the debris of the sixties. So much joy yet malcontent. So many voices raised, then snuffed. My generation's heritage seemed to be in jeopardy.

These things were on my mind: the course of the artist, the course of freedom redefined, the re-creation of space, the emergence of new voices.

And these things I came to express—albeit somewhat awkwardly—through the form of rock and roll. Perhaps I have been none but a scrappy pawn, but I am nonetheless grateful for the moves I came to make.

And salute all who helped me make them.

FIRST SONGS

AND

PERFORMANCE

PIECES

OATH

Jesus died for somebody's sins
but not mine
melting in a pot of thieves
wild card up my sleeve
thick heart of stone
my sins my own
I engrave my own palm
Sweet black X
Adam placed no hex on me
I embrace Eve
and take full responsibility
for every pocket I have picked
mean and slick
every Johnny Ace song I've balled to
long before the church
made it neat and right
So Christ
I'm giving you the good-bye
firing you tonight
I can make my own light shine
and darkness too is equally fine
you got strung up for my brother
but with me I draw the line
you died for somebody's sins
but not mine

WORK SONG

I was working real hard
to show the world
what I could do
oh I guess
I never dreamed
I'd have to
world spins
some photographs
how I love to laugh
when the crowd laughs
while love slips through
a theater that is full
but ooh baby
when the crowd goes home
and I turn in
and I realize I'm alone
I can't believe, I had to
I was working real hard
to show the world
what I could do
oh I guess
I never dreamed
I'd have to
I had to
I had to
sacrifice
you

A FIRE OF UNKNOWN ORIGIN

A fire of unknown origin
Took my baby away
Fire of unknown origin
Took my baby away
Swept her up and off my wavelength
Swallowed her up like the ocean
In a fire thick and gray

Death comes sweeping
Through the hallway
Like a lady's dress
Death comes riding
Down the highway
In its Sunday best
Death comes riding
Death comes creeping
Death comes
I can't do nothing
Death goes
There must be something that remains
Death it made me sick and crazy
'Cause that fire it took my baby away

have you seen
dylans dog
its got wings
it can fly
if you speak
of it to him
its the only time
dylan
cant look you in the eye

goodnight Irene.

have you held dylans snake
it rattles/like a toy
it coils in his hand
it sleeps in the ~~bed~~   he sleepin in the grass
dylans bed   he's the only one
its the only one   stretched out
sleeps near his head   when dylan comes

have you pressed
to your ~~ear~~ face
dylans bird dylans bird
it rolls on the ground   it rests on dylans hip
it sings dylans songs   it drops on dylans ground
its the one   it rolls with him
who can hum like dylan hums   its the only one
                                         who can hum when dylan hums

have you seen
dylans dog   it trembles with him
it's got wings
it can fly   it rests on dylans hump
when it lands   it trembles inside of him
like a clown   it drops upon the ground
its the only thing allowed.   its the only one
look him in the eye   who can hum when dylan hums

Dog Dream, 1971

DOG DREAM

have you seen
dylan's dog
it got wings
it can fly
if you speak
of it to him
it's the only
time dylan
can't look you in the eye

have you seen
dylan's snake
it rattles like a toy
it sleeps in the grass
it coils in his hand
it hums and it strikes out
when dylan cries out
when dylan cries out

have you pressed
to your face
dylan's bird
dylan's bird
it lies on dylan's hip
trembles inside of him
it drops upon the ground
it rolls with dylan 'round
it's the only one
who comes
when dylan comes

have you seen
dylan's dog
it got wings
it can fly
when it lands
like a clown
he's the only
thing allowed
to look dylan in the eye

BALLAD OF A BAD BOY

Oh I was bad
didn't do what I should
mama catch me with a lickin'
and tell me to be good
when I was bad twice times
she shoved me in a hole
and cut off all my fingers
and laid them in a finger bowl

My mama killed me
my papa grieved for me
my little sister Annalea
wept under the almond tree

Oh I loved a car, car
and when I was feelin' sad
I lay down on my daddy's Ford
and I'd feel good
and you know that I got bad
robbed hubcaps from the men
and sold them to the women
and stole them back again
and I got me a car
a Hudson Hornet car
and rolled the pretty ladies
and often went too far

I went to Chicago
I went to Kalamazoo
I went to Nashville

the highways I flew
I went to Salinas
I rode to the sea
and the people all scolded
and pointed to me
they said there's a bad boy

I was so bad boy
they gathered their daughters
I heard what they said
steer away from him, honey
'cause that boy is bad
and tho' he's hung good
and flashes that loot
don't slide by his side
he rides a wrong route
'cause he's a bad boy

I was so bad boy
my mama killed me
my papa grieved for me
my little sister Annalea
wept under the almond tree

And I wept on a stock car
I captured the junkyards
and I sped thru the canyons
though I never went far
from the wreckers mechanics
I worshipped these men
but they laughed at me, man

they called me mama's boy
mama mama mama mama

Monday at midnight
Tuesday at two
drunk on tequila
thinking of you, ma
I drove my car on, ma
wrecking cars was my art
I held a picture of you, ma
close to my heart
I rode closed windows
it was ninety degrees
the crowd it was screaming
it was screaming for me
they said I was nonsense
true diver chicken driver
no sense
but I couldn't hear them
I couldn't see
fenders hot as angels
blazed inside me

I sped on raged in steam heat
I cracked up and rolled at your feet
I rose in flames and rolled in a pit
where you caught me with a tire iron
and covered me in shit
and I coulda got up
but the crowd it screamed no
that boy is evil

too bad for parole
so bad his ma cut off all his fingers
and laid 'em in a finger bowl

His mama killed him
his papa grieved for him
his little sister Annalea
wept under the almond tree

Oh I was bad
didn't do what I should
mama catch me with a lickin'
and she tell me
You be good

—for Sam Shepard

PICTURE HANGING BLUES

Don't hang me up Jesse James
Don't hang me up Jesse James
Too many men have hung me up Jesse James

I know the true story of sweet Jesse James
The picture you have of him is badly framed
He lived as an old man in exchange for his name
He lived in hiding in exchange for his fame

I laid waiting for him on that fateful night
Caring for him though it wasn't right
I knew he was alive
Alive and run free
Another man slain in his place for me
So he could come after me
So he could come and love me

So don't hang me up Jesse James
Don't hang me up Jesse James
Don't hang me up Jesse James
Too many men have hung me

It was Billy the Kid used to lay in my bed
He knew I loved Jesse
It was something I said
I balled Jesse but I had no shame
I balled Billy but I called Jesse's name

Billy traced Jesse
Gun in his hand
Said there's no use living
Half of a man
He begged Jesse kill him
And take up his name
Jesse got the picture
Love was to blame

Billy just trembled
Mouth full of fright
Jesse was left
Love blinding sight
Jesse was hot
Billy was shot
Life was the last thing
That Billy could give
So Jesse could love me
Jesse could live

Billy lay broken
Jesse came slow
And the last words were spoken
Were Jesse James "go!"

And don't hang her up Jesse James
Don't hang her up Jesse James
Don't hang her up Jesse James
Too many men
Yeah, too many men

Jesse James is runnin'
The outlaws all love him
They don't blame him
They say he's a saint
A saint
I ain't sayin' he is
I ain't sayin' he ain't
Though he could live like a man
Love me like a woman
My Billy died like a snake
And Jesse James never came

Oh you hung me up Jesse James
You hung me up Jesse James
And too many men
Too many men have hung me
Up yours Jesse James

vera gemini

Oh your the kind of girl
Id like to find in my mirror
you have all the markings
of the devil girl
yet you are boned like a saint
with the conscience of a snake

Oh your eyes have shifted from me
everyone saw what you did
how you slipped from beneath me.
live a nervous squid
a little false and frigid
the whole crowd knew you did it

yes you have behaved treacherously
and in public too my vera marie
so i believe you'll have to pay

i said you be good or go to hell
in my arms ill be happy to sail you there
my lovely

Oh no more horses horses
were gonna swim like fish
into the hole in which
you planned to ditch me

you have filled me with a vengence
and touched me with your breath
and planned to leave me cold
but you'll never get your wish
im gonna pull you from the dance
you writhe you ride so easily
im gonna gather up your reins in my fist
just me and you
one two
oh no more horses
horses horses

I was your victom
I was well decieved
hells built on regretz
and i hold to many
i love your naked neck
even the lies youve told me
a lily thats bend lying
white and bent and sick

Oh but you arent two faced
you have two faces
that will speak no more no more no more

Oh your the knid of girl
i found in my mirror
laughing
the way you laughed at christ
oh he fell on frid y
rose on monday
but when i take you down you wont rise

The Revenge of Vera Gemini, 1972

THE REVENGE OF VERA GEMINI

You are boned like a saint
with the conscience of a snake

You're the kind of girl
I'd like to find
in my mirror
in my mirror

Your eyes have shifted from me
everyone saw what you did
how you slipped from beneath me
like a nervous squid
a little false and frigid
the whole crowd
knew you did it

Oh no more horses horses
you're going to swim like a fish
into the hole in which
you planned to ditch me

I was your victim
I was well deceived
hell's built on regrets
and I hold too many
I love your naked neck
and the lies you've told me

You aren't two-faced
you have two faces
the face of an angel
with the mark of a devil

You filled me with a vengeance
touched me with your breath
planned to leave me cold
but you'll never get your wish
I'm going to pull you from the dance
you writhe you ride so easily
Gather up the reins with my fist

Oh no more horses horses
you're going to swim like a fish
into the hole in which
you tried to ditch me
my lovely Vera

CAREER OF EVIL

I plot your rubric scarab,
I steal your satellite
I want your wife to be my
Baby tonight, baby tonight

I choose to steal
What you chose to show
And you know
I will not apologize
You're mine for the taking
I'm making a career of evil

Pay me I'll be your surgeon
I'd like to pick your brain
Capture you inject you
Leave you kneeling in the rain
Kneeling in the rain

I choose to steal
What you chose to show
And you know
I will not apologize
You're mine for the taking
I'm making a career of evil

I'd like your blue-eyed horseshoe
I'd like your emerald horny toad
I'll leave all that you value
By the side of the road

And then I'd spend your ransom money,
But still I'd keep your sheep
I'd peel the mask you're wearing
And then rob you of your sleep
Rob you of your sleep

I choose to steal
What you chose to show
And you know
I will not apologize
You're mine for the taking
I'm making a career of evil

—*recorded by Blue Oyster Cult*

Sixteen and time to pay off I got this job in a piss factory inspecting pipe Forty hours thirty-six dollars a week but it's a paycheck, jack. It's so hot in here hot like sahara You could faint in the heat but these bitches are just too lame to understand too goddamn grateful to get this job to know they're getting screwed up the ass.

All these women they got no teeth or gum or cranium And the way they suck hot sausage but me well I wasn't sayin' too much neither I was moral school girl hard-working asshole I figured I was speedo motorcycle had to earn my dough had to earn my dough.

But no you gotta relate, right, you gotta find the rhythm within Floor boss slides up to me and he says Hey sister, you just movin' too fast. You screwin' up the quota. You doin' your piece work too fast. Now you get off your mustang sally, you ain't goin' nowhere, you ain't goin' nowhere.

I lay back. I get my nerve up. I take a swig of romilar and walk up to hot shit Dot Hook and I say Hey, hey sister, it don't matter whether I do labor fast or slow, there's always more labor after. She's real Catholic, see. She fingers her cross and she says There's one reason. There's one reason. You do it my way or I push your face in. We knee you in the john if you don't get off your mustang, Sally, if you don't shake it up baby. Shake it up baby. Twist and shout. Oh would that I could will a radio here. James Brown singing I Lost Someone. Oh the Paragons and the Jesters and Georgie Woods the guy with the goods and Guided Missiles . . . but no, I got nothin', no diversion, no window nothing here but a porthole in the plaster in the plaster where I look down look down at sweet Theresa's convent all those nurses all those nuns scattin' 'round with their bloom hoods like cats in mourning oh to me they look pretty damn free down there down there

piss factory

16 and time to pay off. I got this job in a piss factory
inspecting pipe. sweating my balls off in this hot like
sahara with no windows xxx real bullshit but its a paycheck
you could faint with the heat but the bitches are too lame
to understand they're getting screwed up the ass too god damn
grateful to get this job them with no teeth gripping gum
or cranium.nothing upstairs the way they suck hot sausage
but then i wasnt saying too much neither.i was moral asshole
hard working school girlgotta earn my doe. no. you gotta
play by the rules find the rythumn within them you got to
relate. floor boss says hey you did your piecework to fast
quit screwing up the quota get off your mustang sa,ly you
aint going nowhere.i swig some romalar and get my nerve up
and put it to hot shit Dot Hook, say hey sister i get bored
it dont matter whether you do labor fast or slow theres always
more after. shes no catholic she says there is ONE REASon
chicken do it my way or i push your face in. we may knee ya
in da john if you dont shape up baby. shake it up baby slow
motion inspection is driving me insane. no windows no diversion
would i could will a radio james brown singing I lost someone
hy lit georgie woods the guy with the goods and guided missles.
nothing here save a porthole in the plaster overlooking sweet
teresa convent. nuns in bloom hoods scatting like cats in
mourning. to me they look pretty damn free out there lucky
not to smooth those hands against hot steel free from the
dogma the in-speed of labor. every afternoon like the last
one like re-run lapping up Dot Hooks midwife sweat some
sound track I prefer the way fags smell and spades and dagos
school boys in heat. the way their legs flap under the desk
in study hall and that forbidden acrid lean amonia smell lilacs
the way they droop like dicks.how long am i condemned to pump
my nostrils full of clammy lady. me i refuse to sweat all i
got under my armpits are a few salt lick hairs peeking like pubes
xxxkixx from my sleeveless I refuse to sweat its 110 degrees
in here i refuse to faint they're all waiting but i aintgonna
faint see the monotany is even more brutal hour after hour
in this piss factory more than ever my fists are assembled I
refuse to lose nothing here to hide save desire hide here save
desire. lucky i lifted rimbauds illuminations from the paper
back forum. it was the face on the cover see rimbauds hair
his sailor face. faire than any boy on the block i was seeing.
my salvation my nosegay the words rocked sex smells coming on
like my brothers sheets before the bath what did i care what
he was saying it was the sound the music the way he was saying
it his words over and over in my skull when I was pumping stel
and she was pumping steel we looked the same but i was getting
my first brain fuck illuminations my salvation oh stolen book
no crime since has been so sweet no perfume ever to fill my nose
no snow no more light then the simple knowledge of you rimbaud
sailor face stolen book hidden inside my blouse so close
to my breast.

Piss Factory, 1972

not having to press those smooth not having to smooth those hands against hot steel not having to worry about the inspeed the dogma the inspeed of labor oh they look pretty damn free down there and the way they smell the way the way they smell and here I gotta be up here smellin' Dot Hook's midwife sweat.

I would rather smell the way boys smell oh those schoolboys the way their legs flap under the desk in study hall that odor rising roses and ammonia and the way their dicks droop like lilacs. Or the way they smell that forbidden acrid smell. But no I got a pink clammy lady in my nostril. Her against the wheel me against the wheel Oh slow motion inspection is drivin' me insane in steel next to Dot Hook oh we may look the same shoulder to shoulder sweatin' hundred and ten degrees But I will never faint. They laugh and they expect me to faint but I will never faint I refuse to lose refuse to fall down because you see it's the monotony that's got to me every afternoon like the last one every afternoon like a rerun next to Dot Hook and yeah we look the same both pumpin' steel both sweatin'.

But you know she got nothin' to hide and I got something to hide here called desire I got something to hide here called desire. And I will get out of here you know the fear potion is just about to come. In my nose is the taste of sugar and I got nothin' to hide here save desire And I'm gonna go I'm gonna get out of here I'm gonna get on that train and go to New York City and I'm gonna be somebody I'm gonna get on that train and go to New York City and I'm gonna be so bad. I'm gonna be a big star and I will never return never return no never return to burn at this Piss factory. And I will travel light Oh watch me now.

THE ALBUMS

HORSES

Three chords merged with
the power of the word.

IN EXCELSIS DEO

Jesus died for somebody's sins but not mine
Melting in a pot of thieves wild card up my sleeve
Thick heart of stone my sins my own
They belong to me. Me

People say beware but I don't care
The words are just rules and regulations to me. Me
I walk in a room you know I look so proud
I move in this here atmosphere where anything's allowed
Then I go to this here party but I just get bored
Until I look out the window see a sweet young thing
Humping on the parking meter leaning on the parking meter
Oh, she looks so good. Oh, she looks so fine
And I got this crazy feeling that I'm gonna make her mine

Oh I put my spell on her here she comes
Walking down the street here she comes
Coming through my door here she comes
Crawling up my stair here she comes
Waltzing through the hall in a pretty red dress
And oh, she looks so good. Oh, she looks so fine
And I got this crazy feeling that I'm gonna make her mine

Then I hear this knocking on my door hear this knocking at my door
And I look up at the big tower clock and say oh my God it's midnight
And my baby is walking through the door laying on my couch
She whispers to me and I take the big plunge
And oh, she was so good. And oh, she was so fine
And I'm gonna tell the world that I just made her mine

It was at the stadium. There were twenty thousand girls
Called their names out to me Marie Ruth but to tell you the truth
I didn't hear them. I didn't see. I let my eyes rise to the big tower clock
And I heard those bells chiming in my heart going ding-dong
Ding-dong ding-dong ding-dong ding-dong ding-dong ding-dong
Ding-dong. Calling the time when you came to my room
And you whispered to me and we took the big plunge
And oh, you were so good. Oh, you were so fine
And I've got to tell the world that I made ya mine made ya mine
Made her mine made ya mine made her mine made ya mine

G-L-O-R-I-A Gloria
G-L-O-R-I-A Gloria
G-L-O-R-I-A Gloria

When the tower bells chime
ding-dong they chime
I said that Jesus died
for somebody's sins
but not mine

"Gloria" was bred by crossing the poem "Oath," written in 1970, with the Van Morrison classic. "Gloria" gave me the opportunity to acknowledge and disclaim our musical and spiritual heritage. It personifies for me, within its adolescent conceit, what I hold sacred as an artist. The right to create, without apology, from a stance beyond gender or social definition, but not beyond the responsibility to create something of worth.

REDONDO BEACH

Late afternoon dreaming hotel
We just had the quarrel that sent you away
I was looking for you are you gone gone

Call you on the phone another dimension
Well you never returned oh you know what I mean
I went looking for you are you gone gone

Down by the ocean it was so dismal
Women all standing with shock on their faces
Sad description oh I was looking for you

Everyone was singing girl is washed up
On Redondo Beach and everyone is so sad
I was looking for you are you gone gone

Pretty little girl everyone cried
She was the victim of sweet suicide
I went looking for you are you gone gone

Down by the ocean it was so dismal
Women all standing with shock on their faces
Sad description oh I was looking for you

Desk clerk told me girl was washed up
Was small and angel with apple blonde hair now
I went looking for you are you gone gone

Picked up my key didn't reply
Went to my room started to cry
You were small and angel are you gone gone

Down by the ocean it was so dismal
I was just standing with shock on my face
The hearse pulled away
The girl that had died it was you

You'll never return into my arms
'Cause you are gone gone
Never return into my arms
'Cause you are gone gone
Gone gone gone gone
Good-bye

the women were singing
of a girl who was watched

... Veins full of existance —
.... like the son of a neck Rilce

sad description / but oh I was
listening for   you

Shape of a young man dressed in a coat of
milk

Redondo Beach
it was late afternoon
dreaming Hotel
we had just had the quarrel
that sent you away
I was looking for you-ou
and you were gone gone

called you on the phone
Johnny no answer
never returned
oh you know what I mean mon
I was etc.

down by the ocean it was so dismal
woman standing w/ shock on their faces
Sad description / but oh I was looking
for you —

(Telling
The women were Telling
They turned to tell me
was
up / on Redondo Beach
and everyone was so
sad —

little girl
everyone cried
she was the victom
of sweet suicide

The desk clerk told
me
the girl was
called Johnny
small and
angel
w/ app leblonde
hair

She

Redondo Beach, 1971

His father died and left him a little farm in New England.
All the long black funeral cars left the scene.
And the boy was just standing there alone
Looking at the shiny red tractor
Him and his daddy used to sit inside
And circle the blue fields and grease the night.
It was as if someone had spread butter
On all the fine points of the stars
'Cause when he looked up they started to slip.
Then he put his head in the crux of his arm
And he started to drift, drift to the belly of a ship
Let the ship slide open, and he went inside of it
And saw his daddy behind the control board
Streaming beads of light.
He saw his daddy behind the control board
And he was very different tonight
'Cause he was not human, he was not human.

The little boy's face lit up with such naked joy
That the sun burned around his lids and his eyes were like two suns
White lids, white opals, seeing everything just a little bit too clearly
And he looked around and there was no black ship in sight
No black funeral cars, nothing except for him the raven
And he fell on his knees and looked up and cried out
No, daddy, don't leave me here alone
Take me up, daddy, to the belly of your ship
Let the ship slide open and I'll go inside of it
Where you're not human, you are not human.

But nobody heard the boy's cry of alarm.
Nobody there except for the birds around the New England farm
And they gathered in all directions, like roses they scattered
And they were like compass grass coming together into the head of
A shaman bouquet. Slit in his nose and all the others went shooting
And he saw the lights of traffic beckoning like the hands of Blake
Grabbing at his cheeks, taking out his neck, all his limbs
Everything was twisted and he said:
I won't give up, won't give up, don't let me give up
I won't give up, come here, let me go up fast
Take me up quick, take me up, up to the belly of a ship
And the ship slides open and I go inside of it
Where I am not human.

I am helium raven and this movie is mine
So he cried out as he stretched the sky
Pushing it all out like latex cartoon
Am I all alone in this generation?
We'll just be dreaming of animation night and day
It won't let up, won't let up and I see them coming in
Oh, I couldn't hear them before, but I hear them now
It's a radar scope in all silver and all platinum lights
Moving in like black ships
They were moving in, streams of them
And he put up his hands and he said:
It's me, it's me, I'll give you my eyes, take me up
Oh now please take me up, I'm helium raven
Waiting for you, please take me up, don't leave me here.

The son, the sign, the cross, like the shape of a tortured woman
The true shape of a tortured woman, the mother standing
In the doorway letting her sons, no longer presidents but prophets.
They're all dreaming they're going to bear the prophet
He's going to run through the fields dreaming in animation
It's all going to split his skull, it's going to come out
Like a black bouquet shining, like a fist that's going to shoot them up
Like light, like Mohammed Boxer, take them up up up up up up.
Oh, let's go up up take me up I'll go up I'm going up I'm going up.
Take me up, I'm going up, I'll go up.
Go up go up go up go up up up up up up up
Up, up to the belly of a ship. Let the ship slide open.
We'll go inside of it where we are not human, we are not human.

Where there was sand, there were tiles
The sun had melted the sand and it coagulated like a river of glass
When it hardened he looked at the surface, he saw his face
And where there were eyes were just two white opals, two white opals
Where there were eyes there were just two white opals
And he looked up, and the rays shot, and he saw raven coming in
And he crawled on his back and he went up up up up up up up.
Sha da do wop da shaman do way sha da do wop da shaman do way
Sha da do wop da shaman do way sha da do wop da shaman do way

We like birdland.

FREE MONEY

Every night before I go to sleep
Find a ticket win a lottery
Scoop the pearls up from the sea
Cash them in and buy you
All the things you need

Every night before I rest my head
See those dollar bills go swirling 'round my bed
I know they're stolen but I don't feel bad
I take that money buy you things you never had

Oh baby it would mean so much to me
Oh baby to buy you all the things you need for free

I'll buy you a jet plane baby
Get you on a higher plane to a jet stream
And take you through the stratosphere
And check out the planets there
And then take you down deep deep
Where it's hot hot in Arabia-babia
Then cool cold fields of snow. And we'll roll
Dream roll dream roll roll dream dream

When we dream it when we dream it when we dream it
We'll dream it dream it for free free money free money
Free money free money free money free money

Every night before I go to sleep
Find a ticket win a lottery
Every night before I rest my head
See those dollar bills go swirling 'round my bed

Oh baby it would mean so much to me
Baby I know our troubles will be gone
Oh I know our troubles will be gone going gone
If we dream dream dream for free

And when we dream it when we dream it when we dream it
Let's dream it we'll dream it for free free money free money
Free money free money free money free money free money

KIMBERLY

The wall is high the black barn
The babe in my arms in her swaddling clothes
And I know soon that the sky will split
And the planets will shift
Balls of jade will drop and existence will stop

Little sister the sky is falling
I don't mind I don't mind
Little sister the fates are calling on you

Here I stand again in this old electric whirlwind
The sea rushes up my knees like flame
And I feel like just some misplaced Joan of Arc
And the cause is you looking up at me
Oh baby I remember when you were born
It was dawn and the storm settled in my belly
And I rolled in the grass and I spit out the gas
And I lit a match and the void went flash
And the sky split and the planets hit
Balls of jade dropped and existence stopped

Little sister the sky is falling
I don't mind I don't mind
Little sister the fates are calling on you

I was young and crazy so crazy I knew
I could break through with you
So with one hand I rocked you
And with one heart I reached for you
Ah I knew your youth was for the taking
Fire on a mental plane so I ran through the fields

As the bats with their baby vein faces
Burst from the barn in flames in the violent violet sky
And I fell on my knees and pressed you against me
Your skull was like a network of spittle
Like glass balls moving in like cold streams of logic
And I prayed as the lightning attacked
That something would make it go crack

Something will make it go crack
Something will make it go crack
Something will make it go crack

The palm trees fall into the sea
It doesn't matter much to me
As long as you're safe Kimberly
And I can gaze deep into your starry eyes
Looking deep in your eyes baby
Looking deep in your eyes baby
Looking deep in your eyes baby
Into your starry eyes

BREAK IT UP

Car stopped in a clearing
Ribbon of life, it was nearing
I saw the boy break out of his skin
My heart turned over and I crawled in

He cried break it up, oh, I don't understand
Break it up, I can't comprehend
Break it up, oh, I want to feel you
Don't talk to me that way
I'm not listening

Snow started falling
I could hear the angel calling
We rolled on the ground, he stretched out his wings
The boy flew away and he started to sing

He sang break it up, oh, I don't understand
Break it up, I can't comprehend
Break it up, oh, I want to feel you
Break it up, don't look at me

The sky was raging. The boy disappeared
I fell on my knees. Atmosphere broke up
The boy reappeared. I cried take me please

Ice it was shining. I could feel my heart it was melting
I tore off my clothes, I danced on my shoes
I ripped my skin open and then I broke through, I cried

Break it up, oh, now I understand
Break it up, and I want to go
Break it up, oh, please take me with you
Break it up, I can feel it breaking
I can feel it breaking, I can feel it breaking
I can feel, I can feel, I can feel, I can feel

So break it up, oh, now I'm coming with you
Break it up, now I'm going to go
Break it up, oh, feel me I'm coming
Break it up break it up break it up
Break it up break it up break it up
Break it up break it up break it up

—for Jim Morrison

LAND

All the wisdom of the universe can be
found between the eyes of the horse.

—KORAN

Horses

The boy was in the hallway drinking a glass of tea
From the other end of the hallway a rhythm was generating
Another boy was sliding up the hallway
He merged perfectly with the hallway
He merged perfectly with the mirror in the hallway
The boy looked at Johnny Johnny wanted to run
but the movie kept moving as planned
The boy took Johnny he pressed him against the locker
He drove it in he drove it home he drove it deep in Johnny
The boy disappeared Johnny fell on his knees
started crashing his head against the locker
started crashing his head against the locker
started laughing hysterically
When suddenly Johnny
gets the feeling
he's being surrounded by
horses horses horses horses
coming in all directions
white shining silver studs with their nose in flames
He saw horses horses horses
horses horses horses horses horses

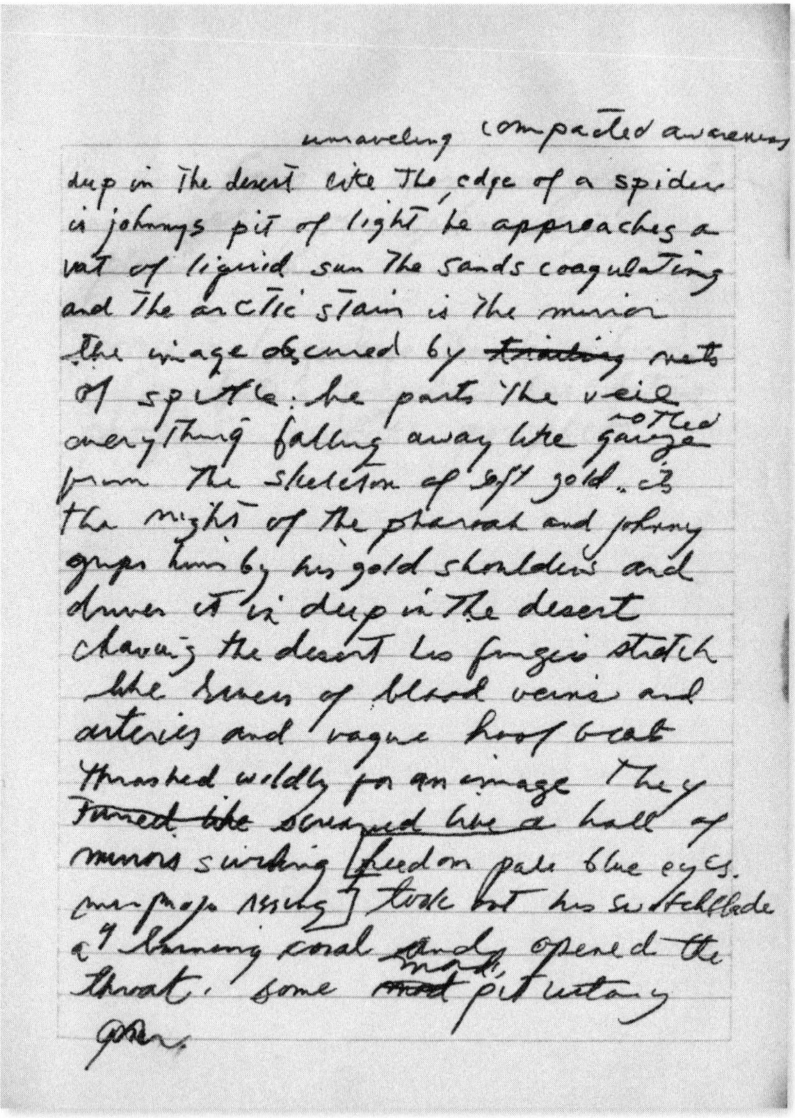
unraveling compacted awareness
deep in the desert like the edge of a spider
is johnnys pit of light he approaches a
vat of liquid sun the sands coagulating
and the arctic stain is the mirror
~~the~~ image obscured by ~~trailing~~ nets
of spittle: he parts the veil
everything falling away like ~~gauze~~ rotted
from the skeleton of soft gold. it's
the night of the pharoah and johnny
grips him by his gold shoulders and
drives it in deep in the desert
clawing the desert his fingers stretch
like rivers of blood veins and
arteries and vague hoof beat
thrashed wildly for an image they
~~turned like~~ screamed like a hall of
mirrors swirling [freedom pale blue eyes
mirages rising] took out his switchblade
of burning coral ~~candy~~ mad opened the
throat. some ~~mad~~ pituitary
gland

Land Genesis, 1973

Land of a Thousand Dances

Do you know how to pony like bony maroney
Do you know how to twist well it goes like this it goes like this
Then you mash potato do the alligator do the alligator
And you twista twista like your baby sister
I want your baby sister give me your baby sister teach your baby sister
To rise up from her knees do the sweet pea do the sweet pee pee
Roll down on her back got to lose control got to lose control
Got to lose control and then you take control
Then you roll down on your back
Do you like it like that like it like that
Then you do the watusi yeah do the watusi
Life is filled with holes Johnny's laying there in his sperm coffin
Angel looks down at him and says ah pretty boy
Can't you show me nothing but surrender
Johnny gets up takes off his leather jacket
Taped to his chest there's the answer
He got pen knives and jack knives and
Switchblades preferred switchblades preferred
He cries he screams says
Life is full of pain I push it through my brain
And I fill my nose with snow and go Rimbaud
Go Rimbaud go Rimbaud oh go Johnny go
And do the watusi oh do the watusi

There's a little place a place called space
It's a pretty little place it's across the track
Across the track and the name of that place
Is I like it like that I like it like that
I like it like that I like it like that

And the name of the band is
Twistelette twistelette twistelette
Twistelette twistelette twistelette

La Mer (de)

Let it calm down let it calm down
In the night in the eye of the forest
There's a mare black and shining with yellow hair
I put my fingers through her silken hair
And found a stair I didn't waste time
I just walked right up and saw that up there
There is a sea up there there is a sea up there
There is a sea seize the possibility
There is no land but the land
[Up there is just a sea of possibilities]
There is no sea but the sea
[Up there is a wall of possibilities]
There is no keeper but the key
[Up there there are several walls of possibilities]
Except for one who seizes possibilities
I seize the first possibility the sea around me
I was standing there with my legs spread like a sailor
[In a sea of possibilities] I felt his hand on my knee
[On the screen] And I looked at Johnny
And handed him a branch of coral flame
[In the heart of man] The waves were coming in
Like Arabian stallions gradually lapping into sea horses

He picked up the blade and he pressed it against
His smooth throat and let it dip in [the veins]
Dip in to the sea the sea of possibilities
It started hardening it started hardening in my hand
And I felt the arrows of desire

I put my hand inside his cranium, oh we had such a brainiac-amour
But no more, no more I gotta move from my mind to the area
[Go Rimbaud go Rimbaud go Rimbaud] Oh go Johnny go
Do the watusi, yeah do the watusi do the watusi
His skull shot open coiled snakes
White and shiny twirling and encircling
Our lives are now entwined we will four years be together
Your nerves the mane of the black shining horse
And my fingers all entwined through your silky hair
I could feel it it was the hair going through my fingers
[Build it build it]
The hairs were like wires going through my body
I that's how I that's how I died
Oh when they made that Tower of Babel
They knew what they were after
They knew what they were after
Everything on the current moved up
I tried to stop it but it was too warm
[No possible ending, no possible ending]
Too unbelievably smooth like playing in the sea
In the sea of possibility the possibility was a blade
A shiny blade I hold the key to the sea of possibilities
There's no land but the land looked at my hands
And there's a red stream that went streaming through

The sands like fingers like arteries like fingers

[All wisdom fixed between the eyes of a horse]

He lay pressing it against his throat [your eyes]

He opened his throat [your eyes] his vocal chords

Started shooting like [of a horse] mad pituitary glands

The scream he made [my heart] was so high

Pitched that nobody heard no one heard

That cry no one heard [Johnny] the butterfly flapping

In his throat his fingers nobody heard he was on that bed

It was like a sea of jelly and so he seized the first

His vocal chords shot up like mad pituitary glands

It was a black tube he felt himself disintegrate

[There is nothing happening at all]

So when he looked out into the street

Saw this sweet young thing

Humping on the parking meter

Leaning on the parking meter

A long Fender whine

In the sheets there was a man

Everything around him unraveling

Like some long Fender whine

Dancing around to a simple rock and roll song

"Land" was an improvisation evoking Chris Kenners's "Land of a Thousand Dances," a salute to the past and an anticipation of the future.

ELEGIE

I just don't know what to do tonight
My head is aching as I drink and breathe
Memory falls like cream in my bones
Moving on my own

There must be something I can dream tonight
The air is filled with the moves of you
All the fire is frozen yet still I have the will

Trumpets, violins, I hear them in the distance
And my skin emits a ray
But I think it's sad, it's much too bad
That all our friends can't be with us today

RADIO ETHIOPIA

Beauty will be convulsive or not at all.

—ANDRÉ BRETON, *NADJA*

Reprinted courtesy of The Yipster Times *(March-April, 1977). A subscription to* The Yipster Times *is only $6/yr. to
P.O. Box 392, Canal Street Station, New York, NY 10013. The Patti Smith Group's new record is* Radio Ethiopia *on Arista Records.
Patti says: "*Radio Ethiopia *goes beyond the wax into a disc of light. Fight the good fight."*

You Can't Say "Fuck" in Radio Free America

BY PATTI SMITH

*New Year's Eve, Patti Smith gave a concert at NYC's Palladium. WNEW-FM refused to air the concert on their station due to her using the
word "fuck" on an interview with the station last November. Upon hearing of this decision, Patti wrote this heavy condemnation of "progressive"
rock radio as we hear it now.*

Fuck the word...fuck the word
fuck the word the word is dead
is re-defined...the bird in the (womb)
is expelled by the propelling
motion of fuck of fucking

On November 29, Patti Smith delivered an address
on WNEW-FM in New York City. Because of the content
of this message, the Patti Smith Group will not be aired
live in the future on Metromedia. A transcript is avail-
able to the people, for the people who support free
communication to decide what programming they want
to hear on their radio. (S.a.s.e. to Radio Ethiopia, P.O.
Box 188, Mantua, New Jersey 08051).
THE RESISTANCE
We believe in the total freedom of communication
and we will not be compromised. The censorship of
words is as meaningless as the censorship of musical
notes; we cannot tolerate either. Freedom means exact-
ly that: no limits, no boundaries...rock and roll is not
a colonial power to be exploited, told what to say and
how to say it. This is the spirit in which our music
began and the flame in which it must be continued.
Radio Ethiopia is a symphony of experience...each
piece a movement...14 movements...14 stations.

There is silence on my radio...
-Stones
They are trying to silence us, but they cannot
succeed. We cannot be "trusted" not to pollute the
airwaves with our idealism and intensity. W(New)
York radio has proved unresponsive at best to the
new rock and roll being born under its ears...a music
having worldwide cause and effect...injecting a new
sense of urgency and imperative. Radio has consist-
ently lagged behind the needs of the community it
is honor-bound to serve. We do not consider patern-
alistic token airplay and passive coverage to be enough.
FM radio was birthed in the 1960's as an alternative to

restrictive playlisting and narrow monopolistic visions.
The promise is being betrayed.

We Want The Radio And We Want It Now
1977...the celebration of 1776-1976 ends tonight...
we end with the same desires of individual and ethnic
freedom of concept...the freedom of art...the freedom
of work...the freedom/flow of energy that keeps re-
building itself with the nourishment of each generation.
The political awareness of the 1960's was a result of the
political repression of the 1950's. The 70's have rep-
resented the merging of both...political-artistic/activism-
expression.
The colonial year is dead. Rock and roll is not a
colonial art. We colonize to further the freedom
of space.

We must dedicate ourselves to the future...in the
sixties the DOG was GOD...the underdogs rose
up and merged and fought for political freedom...
we of 1977 are Rat/Art.
—Radio Ethiopia, 1977

suspended in relics (art)...The guardians of ritual salute
all that heralds and redefines civilization into a long
streaming system of tongues...salute then spit on those
who left us the ruins of much broken ground then move
on...

dedicated to the future we are thus fasting...we rip
into the past/perfect like raw meat...we do not accept
the past as the summit of creation...we rise and pierce
the membrane of mire and waste...the stagnation of
rust...

1977. We the people of the neo-army are spewing
JUST LUST...The absolute motion into the future...
To fight the good fight...the fight for freedom of ex-
pression...The fight against fat and Roman satisfaction.

WE DON'T WANT NO SATISFACTION
!!THE ART/RAT DAWNS!!
(THE AWAKENING GRAIN)

RAISE UP! TAKE POSITION/ DUO-SONIC THE
SYSTEM OF GOD. ILLUMINATED WEAPONS
POISED LIKE MALLOTS LIKE 2-SOUND PICK-UPS
BAYONETING THE FLESH OF THE EYE...A GRAIN
OF SAND THRU THE OPTIC NERVES OF HE THAT
SEIZE ALL...A-R (rasive) AND STONED AND IR-
RATED BY A SPECT(RE) SO CUNNING HE EVEN-
TUALLY SHOWS HIS PHASE HE EVENTUALLY
WAKES UP) (SHARP AND ROUGH AND DELICATE-
LY CUT THE AWAKENING GRAIN DOES ITS
WORK! THE ART/RAT DAWNS AGAIN! ART/RAT
KNAWS THRU SPACE/ RUSHING TADPOLES/ A
BLACK STREAK ACROSS THE WHITE HOTEL...
THE GLASS THAT SEPARATES HIM FROM
SOCIETY IS THE TRUE PRISON OF LIGHT...ART/
RAT IN THE SHAPE OF A BOY DRESSED IN A
COAT OF MILK...ACTION PAINTER...RUBEDO
HAIR OF THE ONE WHO SOARS AND SLASHES
THRU THE AVIATOR BACK/FLAP W/OUT BAR-
ING THE SENCE OF PURE TONGUE RYTHUM...
ART/RAT POSSESING THE NOBEL CONCEIT OF
THE FUTURE AWAITS HIGH ORDERS TO SPEW
THE TONGUE OF LOVE THAT UTTERS THE MOST
PRECIOUS COMMAND THE WORDS OF LOVE THAT
TURN US ON (THE PHYSICAL HIEROGLYPHICS)
)(THE 14 POSITIONS) ARE "FUCK ME FUCK ME
FUCK ME FUCK ME...FUCK THE WORD/ THE
WORD IS DEAD/ FUCK IS DEAD ON THE RADIO/
THE WORD IS DEAD/ IN A WAVE OF SOUND/ TO
BE UNBOUND AND WAVED AND DEFILED LIKE
A BANNER OUTSIDE SOCIETY OVER THE BLACK
RIVER...CITIZENS ARISE! SPIT—BALL INTO"THE
SKY! THE AWAKENING GRAIN AWAKENING
A—WAKE UP W

ASK THE ANGELS

Move. Ask the angels who they're calling
Go ask the angels if they're calling to thee
Ask the angels, while they're falling
Who that person could possibly be

And I know you got the feeling
You know, I feel it crawl across the floor
And I know, it got you reeling
And honey, honey the call is for war
And it's wild, wild, wild, wild

Across the country through the fields
You know I see it written 'cross the sky
People rising from the highway
And war, war is the battle cry
And it's wild, wild, wild, wild

Armageddon, it's gotten
No Savior jailer can take it from me
World ending, it's just beginning
And rock and roll is what I'm born to be
And it's wild, wild, wild, wild

Ask the angels if they're starting to move
Coming in droves in from L.A.
Ask the angels if they're starting to groove
Light as our armor and it's today
And it's wild, wild, wild, wild

Ain't It Strange, 1976

AIN'T IT STRANGE

Down in Vineland there's a clubhouse
Girl in white dress boy shoot white stuff
Oh don't you know that anyone can join
And they come and call and they fall on the floor
Don't you see when you're looking at me
That I'll never end transcend transcend
Ain't it strange oh oh oh
Ain't it strange oh oh oh
Come and join me I implore thee
I implore thee come explore me
Oh don't you know that anyone can come
And they come and they call and they crawl on the floor
Don't you see when you're looking at me
That I'll never end transcend transcend
Ain't it strange oh oh oh
Ain't it strange oh oh oh
True true who are you
Who who am I

Down in Vineland there's a clubhouse
Girl in white dress boy shoot white stuff
Oh don't you know anyone can come
And they come and call and they fall on the floor
Don't you see when you're looking at me
That I'll never end transcend transcend
Ain't it strange oh oh oh
Ain't it strange oh oh oh

do you go to the temple tonight oh no i don't think so do you not
go to the palace of answers with me marie oh no i don't think so no
see when they offer me book of gold i know soon still that platinum

is coming and when i look inside of your temple it looks just like the
inside of any one man and when he beckons his finger to me well i
move in another direction i move in another dimension i move in
another dimension oh oh oh

Hand of God I feel the finger
Hand of God I start to whirl
Hand of God I do not linger

Don't get dizzy do not fall now
Turn whirl like a dervish
Turn God make a move
Turn Lord I don't get nervous
I just move in another dimension
Come move in another dimension
Come move in another dimension
Come move in another dimension
Strange strange

do you go to the temple tonight oh no i don't think so no will you
go to the pagoda the palace of answers with me marie oh no i don't
believe so no see when they offer me book of gold i know soon still
that platinum is coming and when i look inside your temple it looks
just like the inside of the brain of any one man and when he beckons
his finger to me well i move in another dimension i move in another
dimension i move in another dimension

Heard it on the radio it's no good
Heard it on the radio it's news to me
When she getting something it's understood
Baby's got something she's not used to
Down down poppy yeah
Waiting on the corner wanna score
Baby wants something she's in the mood to
Baby wants something I want more
When I don't get it I get blue blue
Down down and it's really coming
Really coming down down poppy yeah

She was tense and gleaming in the sun
They split her open like a country
Everyone was very pleased to be a state of
Her mind was gently probed like a finger
Everything soaking and spread with butter
And then they laid her on the table
She connected with the inhaler
And the needle was shifting like crazy
She was she was completely still
It was like a painting of a vase
She just lay there and the gas traveled fast
Thru the dorsal spine and down and around
The anal cavity her cranium it was really great man
The gas had inflicted her entire spine
With the elements of a voluptuous disease
With a green vapor made her feet light
I moved thru the door I saw the wheel and it was golden
And oh my God I finally scored
I turned the channel station after station

I don't think there's any station
Quite as interesting to me as the 12th station
I tuned in to the tower too many centuries
Were calling to me spinning down thru time
Oh watch them say you're too high
Before him we didn't worship suffering
Didn't we laugh and dance for hours
We were having fun as we built the tower
I saw it spiraling up into his electric eye
I felt it go in and started to cry
Oh God are you afraid
Why did the tower turn you off babe
I want to feel you in my radio
Goddamn in my radio
If you want to go go if you want to see
If you want to go as far as she
You must look God in the face
Heard it on the radio heard it on the radio
One long ecstatic pure sensation restriction started excreting
Started excreting ah exhilarating bottomless pit
Hey Sheba hey Salome hey Venus eclipsing my way ah
You're vessel every woman is a vessel is evasive is aquatic
Everyone silver ecstatic platinum disk spinning

PISSING IN A RIVER

Pissing in a river watching it rise
Tattoo fingers shy away from me
Voices voices mesmerize
Voices voices beckoning sea
Come come come come back come back
Come back come back come back

Spoke of a wheel tip of a spoon
Mouth of a cave I'm a slave I'm free
When are you coming hope you come soon
Fingers fingers encircling thee
Come come come come come come
Come come come come come come for me

My bowels are empty excrete in your soul
What more can I give you baby I don't know
What more can I give you to make this thing grow
Don't turn your back now I'm talking to you
Should I pursue a path so twisted
Should I crawl defeated and gifted
Should I go the length of a river
The royal the throne the cry me river

Everything I've done I've done for you
Oh I give my life for you
Every move I made I move to you
And I came like a magnet for you now

What about it you're going to leave me
What about it you don't need me
What about it I can't live without you
What about it I never doubted you
What about it what about it
What about it what about it

Should I pursue a path so twisted
Should I crawl defeated and gifted
Should I go the length of a river
The royal the throne the cry me river
What about it what about it what about it
Oh I'm pissing in a river

spoke of a wheel
Tip of a spoon
Tongue extending
I'm a slave / I'm free
pressure lingers
here me sigh
Fingers fingers
Encircle Thee

in The night
in The ~~light~~ eye
of The

my bowels are empty
excrete in your soul
what more can I give you
Baby I don't know
Blood in The river
hard celluloid
~~This my head to a ball~~
~~The move~~
film on my body
I'm shooting for you

Oh I'm SiNKing
Sweet gravity

Pissing in a River, 1976

DISTANT FINGERS

When when will you be landing
When when will you return
Feel feel my heart expanding
You and your alien arms

All my earthly dreams are shattered
I'm so tired I quit
Take me forever it doesn't matter
Deep inside of your ship
La la la la la la landing
Please oh won't you return
See your blue lights are flashing
You and your alien arms

Deep in the forest I whirl
Like I did as a little girl
Let my eyes rise in the sky
Looking for you oh you know
I would go anywhere at all
'Cause no star is too far with you

La la la la la la landing
Please oh won't you return
Feel feel my heart expanding
You and your alien arms

All my earthly dreams are shattered
I'm so tired I quit
Take me forever it doesn't matter
Deep inside of your ship

Land land oh I am waiting for you
Waiting for you to take me up by my starry spine
With your distant distant fingers
Oh I am waiting for you
Oh I am waiting for you

PUMPING (MY HEART)

Oh I see your stare spiraling up there
Into the center of my brain and baby come baby go
And free the hurricane oh I go into the center of the airplane
Baby gotta move to the center of my pain
And my heart starts pumping my fists start pumping
Upset total abandon upset you know I love you so
Upset total abandon
Oh I see you stare spiraling up there and oh
Into the center of my brain and baby come baby go
And free the hurricane oh I go into the center of the airplane
Baby gotta box in the center of the ring
And my heart starts pumping my fists start pumping
Upset total abandon you know I love you so
Total abandon oh I go into the center of the airplane
Baby gotta go to the center of my brain
And my heart starts pumping my fists start pumping
Got no recollection of my past reflection
So I'm free to move in the resurrection
My heart starts pumping my fists start pumping
My heart pumping my heart pumping my heart pumping
Coming in the airport coming in the sea coming in the garden
Got a conscious stream coming in a washroom coming on a plane
Coming in a force field coming in my brain and my heart
My heart total abandon total abandon total abandon total
Abandon total abandon total abandon total abandon
Oh I go into the center of the airplane
Baby gotta move to the center of my brain
My heart

CHIKLETS

last night i awoke up from a dream came face to face with my face facing the tombstone teeth of a man called chiklets he came down through the ages with the desperate beauty of a middleweight boxer came beating the force field with elegant grace trying to get a perfect grip there was no absolute grip he was in a sail boat a glass bottom boat the bottom of a boat he was coming down through the ages sea molten sea spilling down the tube the spiny eye of the village the spinal eye of the victim the spiny eye like a question mark hovering over him what do you want what do you want from him down on a dream too much unexplained what do you think do you think there was an actual connection i can't imagine a connection going down there i can't imagine any connection at all a box-ing ring with gold ropes soft desperate karat top spinning and coming down through the ages forty one BC

Oh I'll send you a telegram
Oh I have some information for you
Oh I'll send you a telegram
Send it deep in the heart of you
Deep in the heart of your brain is a lever
Deep in the heart of your brain is a switch
Deep in the heart of your flesh you are clever
Oh honey you met your match in a bitch
There will be no famine in my existence
I merge with the people of the hills
People of Ethiopia
Your opiate is the air that you breathe
All those mint bushes around you
Are the perfect thing for your system
Aww clean clean it out
You must rid yourself from these these animal fixations
You must release yourself
From the thickening blackmail of elephantiasis
You must divide the wheat from the rats
You must turn around and look oh God
When I see Brancusi
His eyes searching out the infinite
Abstract spaces in the radio
Rude hands of sculptor
Now gripped around the neck of a Duo-Sonic
I swear on your eyes no pretty words will sway me

Ahh look at me look at the world around you
Jesus I hate to laugh but I can not believe
Care I so much everything merges then touch it
With a little soul anything is possible
Ahhh I never knew you how can it be
That I feel so fucked up
I am in no condition to do what I must do
The first dog on the street can tell you that
As for you you do as you must
But as for me I trust
That you will book me on the first freighter
Passage on the first freighter
So I can get the hell out of here
And go back home back to Abyssinia
Deep in the heart of the valley I'm going
Ohhh I would appreciate if you would just
Totally appreciate Brancusi's Bird in Space
The sculptor's mallet has been replaced
By the neck of a guitar
Lately
Every time I see your face
I eventually
wake up

EASTER

Use menace, use prayer.

—JEAN GENET

'TILL VICTORY

Raise the sky, we got to fly
Over the land over the sea
Fate unwinds and if we die souls arise
God, do not seize me please. 'Till victory

Take arm. Take aim. Be without shame
No one to bow to. To vow to. To blame
Legions of light virtuous flight ignite excite
And you will see us coming
V formation through the sky
Film survives. Eyes cry. On the hill
Hear us call through a realm of sound
Oh oh-oh down and down
Down and 'round oh down and 'round
'Round and 'round oh 'round and 'round

Rend the veil and we shall sail
The nail. The grail. That's all behind thee
In deed in creed the curve of our speed
And we believe that we will raise the sky
We got to fly over the land over the sea
Fate unwinds and if we die souls arise
God, do not seize me please. 'Till victory
Victory. 'Till victory. Victory. 'Till victory

Blood on the TV ten o'clock news.
Souls are invaded heart in a groove
Beating and beating so out of time
What's the mad matter with the church chimes
Here comes a stranger up on Ninth Avenue
Leaning green tower indiscreet view
Over the cloud over the bridge
Sensitive muscle sensitive ridge
Of my space monkey sign of the time-time
Space monkey so out of line-line
Space monkey son of divine
And he's mine mine all mine

Pierre Clemente. Snortin' cocaine.
The sexual streets why it's all so insane
Humans are running lavender room
Hovering liquid move over moon
For my space monkey sign of the time-time
Space monkey son of divine
Space monkey so out of line
And he's mine mine oh he's mine

Stranger comes up to him
Hands him an old rusty Polaroid
It starts crumbling in his hands.
He says, oh man, I don't get the picture
This is no picture this is just this just a this just a . . .
Just my jack-knife just my jack-knife just my jack.

Rude excavation. Landing site.
Boy hesitating jack-knife
He rips his leg open so out of time
Blood and light running
It's all like a dream
Light of my life he's dressed in flame
It's all so predestined it's all such a game
For my space monkey sign of the time-time
Space monkey son of divine space monkey
So out of line and it's all just space just space

There he is up in a tree.
Oh, I hear him calling down to me
That banana-shaped object ain't no banana
It's a bright yellow UFO and he's coming to get me
Here I go up up up up up up up up
Oh, good-bye mama I'll never do dishes again
Here I go from my body
Ha Ha Ha Ha Ha Ha
Help

BECAUSE THE NIGHT

Take me now baby here as I am
Pull me close, try and understand
Desire is hunger is the fire I breathe
Love is a banquet on which we feed

Come on now try and understand
The way I feel when I'm in your hands
Take my hand come undercover
They can't hurt you now, can't hurt you now

Because the night belongs to lovers
Because the night belongs to love
Because the night belongs to lovers
Because the night belongs to us

Have I doubt when I'm alone
Love is a ring, the telephone
Love is an angel, disguised as lust
Here in our bed, until the morning comes

Come on now try and understand
The way I feel under your command
Take my hand as the sun descends
They can't touch you now, can't touch you now

And though we're seized with doubt
The vicious circle turns and burns
Without you I cannot live, forgive
The yearning burning, I believe it's time
To feel to heal, so touch me now
Touch me now, touch me now

Because this night there are two lovers
Because we believe in the night we trust
Because the night belongs to lovers
Because the night belongs to us

—Cowritten with Bruce Springsteen

GHOST DANCE

What is it children that falls from the sky
Tayi taya tayi aye aye
Manna from heaven from the most high
Food from the father tayi taya aye
We shall live again we shall live again
Shake out the ghost dance

Peace to your brother, give and take eat
Tayi taya dance little feet
One foot extended snake to the ground
Wave up the earth worm turn around
We shall live again we shall live again
Shake out the ghost dance

Stretch out your arms now dip and sway
Bird of thy birth tayi taya
The oe of the shoe the ou of the soul
Dust of the word that shakes from the tail
We shall live again we shall live again
Shake out the ghost dance

Here we are, Father your Holy Ghost
Bread of your bread host of your host
We are the tears that fall from your eyes
Word of your word cry of your cry
We shall live again we shall live again

What is it Father
That moves in the night
What is it Father
That snakes to the right
What is it Father
That shakes from your hand
What is it Father
Can you tell me when
Father will we live again
We shall live again
We shall live again
We shall live again
Shake out the ghost

everything is shit.. the word ART must
be redefined. this is the age where
everybody creates.. rise up nigger take
up your true place.. rise up nigger the
word too must be redefined. this is
your arms and this is your hook. don8t
the black boys get shook. high asses
asses get down. NIGGER no invented for
xhhe color it was made for the plague.
for the royalty who have readjusted
their sores.. the artist. the mutant,.
xthe rock and roll mulatto,. arise new,
babe born sans eye-brow and tonsil..
outside logic beyond mathmatics
self torture and poli-tricks.. the
new science advances unknown geometry.
arise with new eyes new kaath health
new niggers.. this is your call your
calling your psalm.rise up niggers
and reign with your instruments
soldiers of new fortune.uncalcuable
caste of we new niggers.

          MADE FOR the PLAGUE

Manifesto notes, 1977

BABELOGUE

i haven't fucked much with the past, but i've fucked plenty with the future over the skin of silk are scars from the splinters of stations and walls i've caressed. a stage is like each bolt of wood, like a log of helen, is my pleasure. i would measure the success of a night by the way by the way by the amount of piss and seed i could exude over the columns that nestled the PA some nights i'd surprise everybody by skipping off with a skirt of green net sewed over with flat metallic circles which dazzled and flashed. the lights were violet and white i had an ornamental veil, but i couldn't bear to use it. when my hair was cropped i craved covering, but now my hair itself is a veil, and the scalp of a crazy and sleepy comanche lies beneath this netting of skin. i wake up. i am lying peacefully. i am lying peacefully and my knees are open to the sun. i desire him, and he is absolutely ready to seize me. in heart i am moslem in heart i am an american. in heart i am moslem. in heart i'm an american artist and i have no guilt. i seek pleasure. i seek the nerves under your skin. the narrow archway; the layers; the scroll of ancient lettuce. we worship the flaw, the belly, the belly, the mole on the belly of an exquisite whore. he spared the child and spoiled the rod. i have not sold myself to god.

Baby was a black sheep baby was a whore
Baby got big and baby get bigger
Baby get something baby get more
Baby baby baby was a rock n roll nigger
Oh look around you all around you
Riding on a copper wave
Do you like the world around you
Are you ready to behave
Outside of society they're waiting for me
Outside of society that's where I want to be

Baby was a black sheep baby was a whore
You know she got big. Well she's gonna get bigger
Baby got a hand got a finger on the trigger
Baby baby baby is a rock n roll nigger
Outside of society that's where I want to be
Outside of society they're waiting for me

Those who have suffered understand suffering
And thereby extend their hand
The storm that brings harm
Also makes fertile blessed is the grass
And herb and the true thorn

I was lost in a valley of pleasure
I was lost in the infinite sea
I was lost and measure for measure
Love spewed from the heart of me

I was lost and the cost
And the cost didn't matter to me
I was lost and the cost
Was to be outside society
Jimi Hendrix was a nigger
Jesus Christ and grandma too
Jackson Pollock was a nigger
Nigger nigger nigger nigger
Nigger nigger nigger
Outside of society they're waiting for me
Outside of society if you're looking
That's where you'll find me
Outside of society they're waiting for me

WE THREE

Every Sunday I would go down to the bar where he played guitar
You say you want me. I want another. Say you dream of me

Dream of your brother. Oh, the stars shine so suspiciously for we three
You said when you were with me that nothing made you high
We drank all night together and you began to cry so recklessly
Baby please don't take my hope away from me
You say you want me. I want another baby

You say you wish for me. Wish for your brother
Oh, the dice roll so deceptively for we three
It was just another Sunday and everything was in the key of A
And I lit a cigarette for your brother
And he turned and heard me say so desperately
Baby please don't take my hope away from me

You say you want me. I want another
You say you pray for me. Pray for your brother
Oh, the way that I see him is the way I see myself
So please stand back now and let time tell
Oh, can't you see that time is the key
That will unlock the destiny of we three

Every night on separate stars before we go to sleep we pray
So breathlessly. Baby please don't take my hope away from me

what i feel when i'm playing guitar is completely cold and
crazy like i don't owe nobody nothing and it's just a test just to
see how far I can and relax into the cold wave of a note when
everything hits just right the note of nobility can go on forever i
never tire of the solitary E and i trust my guitar and i don't care
about anything sometimes i feel like i've broken through and
i'm free and i could dig into eternity riding the wave and realm
of the E sometimes it's useless here I am struggling and filled
with dread afraid that i'll never squeeze enough graphite from
my damaged cranium to inspire or asphyxiate any eyes grazing
like hungry cows across the stage or page inside of me i'm crazy
i'm just crazy inside i must continue i see her my stiff muse jut-
ting around 'round 'round 'round like a broken speeding statue
the colonial year is dead and the greeks too are finished the
face of alexander remains not only solely due to sculpture but
through the power and foresight and magnetism of alexander
himself the artist must maintain his swagger he must be intoxi-
cated by ritual as well as result look at me i am laughing I'm
like the hard brown palm of the boxer and i trust my guitar
therefore we black out together therefore i would run through
scum and scum is just ahead we see it but we just laugh we're
ascending through the hollow mountain we are peeking we are
laughing we are kneeling we are radiating at last this rebellion
is just a gas our gas that we pass

TWENTY-FIFTH FLOOR

We explore the men's room
we don't give a shit
ladies' lost electricity
take vows inside of it
desire to dance
too startled to try
wrap my legs 'round you
starting to fly let's explore
up there, up there, up there
on the twenty-fifth floor

Circle all around me
coming for the kill
kill kill oh kill me baby
like a kamikaze
heading for a spill
oh but it's all spilt milk to me
desire to dance
too startled to try
wrap my legs 'round you
starting to fly let's soar
up there, up there, up there
on the twenty-fifth floor

We do not eat flower of creation
we do not eat eat anything at all
love is, love was
love is a manifestation
I'm waiting for a contact to call.
love's war. love's cruel. love's pretty
love's pretty cruel tonight

I'm waiting here to refuel
I'm gonna make contact tonight
blood in my heart. Night to exploit
twenty-five stories over Detroit
and there's more
up there, up there, up there

Stoned in space. Zeus. Christ. it has always been rock and so
it is and so it shall be. within the context of neo rock we must
open up our eyes and seize and rend the veil of smoke which
man calls order. pollution is a necessary result of the inability
of man to reform and transform waste. the transformation of
waste is perhaps the oldest pre-occupation of man. man being
the chosen alloy, he must be reconnected via shit, at all cost.
inherent within us is the dream of the task of the alchemist
to create from the clay of man and re-create from excretion of
man pure and then soft and then solid gold. all must not be art.
some art we must disintegrate. positive anarchy must exist.

I feel it swirling around me
I feel I'm feeling no pain
I'm waiting above for you baby
I know that I'll see you up there
I'm tripping in the dark backward
I'm going for all that it's worth
I'm waiting above in the sky dear
upon another planet called earth

EASTER

Easter Sunday we were walking
Easter Sunday we were talking
Isabelle, my little one
Take my hand time has come

Isabelle, all is glowing
Isabelle, all is knowing
And my heart, Isabelle
And my head, Isabelle

Frédéric and Vitalie
Savior dwells inside of thee
Oh, the path leads to the sun
Brother sister time has come

Isabelle, all is glowing
Isabelle, all is knowing
Isabelle, we are dying
Isabelle, we are rising

I am the spring
the holy ground
I am the seed
Of mystery
the thorn the veil
the face of grace
the brazen image
the thief of sleep
the ambassador of dreams
the prince of peace

I am the sword
the wound the stain
scorned transfigured
child of Cain
I rend I end
I return again
I am the salt
the bitter laugh
I am the gas
in a womb of light
The evening star
the ball of sight
That bleeds that sheds
the tears of Christ
Dying and drying
as I rise tonight

Isabelle, we are rising
Isabelle, we are rising
Isabelle, we are rising

—for Arthur, Vitalie, and Isabelle Rimbaud

GODSPEED

You are the adrenaline rushing through my veins
Stimulate my heart pale and crystalline
You are the sulfur extinguished by the flame
You are everything to me, all this in your name

Walking in your blue coat, weeping admiral
All the twisted sailors, Vienna and Genet
Ending all that's static in a myth of sin
Mirror mine ecstatic pale adrenaline

Love is a vampire, energy undead
Love is like a boomerang, gone and back again
On a rack of red leather, on a rack of skin and sin
Tell me how to sail sail sail pale adrenaline

And you said to me it could never be
Sent me out to sea to see
And you said Godspeed

Follow follow me down the twisted stair
Stuck inside a memory shot and shot again
Hand upon a railing courting fate and fate
Down a black river and I plunge right in

Adrenaline move inside my vein
Ah, you're the speed I need throw the pistol in
Love is like a vampire coming in to suck suck
I fell and fell and fell and I'm going to duck

WAVE

I have fought a good fight,
I have finished my course.

—TIMOTHY 4:7

FREDERICK

Hi hello awake from thy sleep
God has given your soul to keep
All of the power that burns in the flame
Ignites the light in a single name

Frederick, name of care
Fast asleep in a room somewhere
Guardian angels lay abed
Shed their light on my sleepy head

High on a threshold yearning to sing
Down with the dancers having one last fling
Here's to the moment when you said hello
Come into my spirit are you ready let's go

Hi hi hey hey maybe I will
Come back some day now
But tonight on the wings of a dove
Up above to the land of love

Now I lay me down to sleep
Pray the Lord my soul to keep
Kiss to kiss, breath to breath
My soul surrenders astonished to death

Night of wonder promise to keep
Set our sails channel the deep
Capture the rapture, two hearts meet
Combined entwined in a single beat

Frederick, you're the one
As we journey from sun to sun
All the dreams I waited so long for
Our flight tonight so long so long

Bye bye hey hey maybe
We will come back some day now
But tonight on the wings of a dove
Up above to the land of love

Frederick, name of care
High above with sky to spare
All the things I've been dreaming of
All expressed in this name of love

dream of linda

Frederick

       end the song
Til the stars are gone

2 | I'm w/ the dancers having
one last fling
I'm on the threshold
yearning to sing

1 | Guardian angels
up in the sky
cease w/ your Trumpets
hear my cry
I am so a
this is what I've
wanted goodbye So long

3 | Bye bye
hey hey

4 | Frederick
name of care
high alone in a ~~storm~~

Ⓕ waiting for ~~so long~~
~~goodbye~~ so long

Frederick, 1978

She is benediction
She is addicted to thee
She is rude connecting w/ he
a connection

she is benediction
she is addicted to thee
she is the rude connection
she is connecting w/ he
here al go well al don't know why
I spin so sencelesly
Could it be he's taken over me
I'm dancing barefoot
heading for a spin
some strange music draws me
in / makes me come on
like some heroine

She is consecration
~~She is the essence~~ .
She is concentrating on thee
she is slow sensation
streaming the essence of he
here I come well I don't know
why, spend
I ~~film~~ so ceacelessly
could it be he's taken
over me

Dancing Barefoot, 1978

DANCING BAREFOOT

She is benediction
She is addicted to thee
She is the rude connection
She is connecting with he

Here I go and I don't know why
I spin so ceaselessly
Could it be he's taking over me
I'm dancing barefoot
Heading for a spin
Some strange music draws me in
Makes me come on like some heroine

She is sublimation
She is the essence of thee
She is concentrating on he
Who is chosen by she

Here I go and I don't know why
I spin so ceaselessly
Could it be he's taking over me
I'm dancing barefoot
Heading for a spin
Some strange music draws me in
Makes me come on like some heroine

She is re-creation
She, intoxicated by thee
She has the slow sensation
That he is levitating with she

Here I go and I don't know why
I spin so ceaselessly
'Till I lose my sense of gravity
I'm dancing barefoot
Heading for a spin
Some strange music draws me in
Makes me come on like some heroine

Oh God, I fell for you
Oh God, I fell for you
Oh God, I feel the fever
Oh God, I feel the pain
Oh God, forever after
Oh God, I'm back again
Oh God, I fell for you
Oh God, I fell for you

REVENGE

I feel upset. Let's do some celebrating
Come on honey don't hesitate now
Needed you. You withdrew. I was so forsaken
Ah, but now the tables have turned. My move
I believe I'll be taking my revenge. Sweet revenge

I thought you were some perfect read-out. Some digital delay
Had obscured and phased my view of the wicked hand you played
The sands and hands of time have run out. Run out
You better face it this thing's run amok. This luck
I do know how to replace it with revenge. Sweet revenge

I gave you a wristwatch baby
You wouldn't even give me the time of day
You want to know what makes me tick
Now it's me that's got precious little to say
For the ghosts of our love have dried have died
There's no use faking it
The spirits going to close in on you tonight
High time I was taking my revenge
Sweet revenge. Revenge. Revenge

All the gold and silver couldn't measure
Up my love for you. It's so immaterial
I wouldn't wait around if I were you
In the valley of wait-ting ting
Nobody gets nothing. Nobody gets anything.
No time for kisses
Don't leave me no space in your little boat
You ain't going to need, no you ain't going to need no little boat
You are living on marked time my dear. Revenge. Sweet revenge.
Sweet, sweet revenge.

 Aint got a passport
Aint got a real name
Ain got a chance spot
as fortune or fame
and so I walk these empty streets
won't you give me a lift
a lift / a lift
on som Citizenship

They were rioting in Chicago
movement in L.a,
1968 broke the Yardbirds
were were broke as well
took it underground
MC Borderline
Up against the wall
the wall / the wall
show your papers boy

~~the came~~ unmarried
~~the came~~ New York City
~~the~~ entered her embrace
~~no work nowhere~~ to sleep
So we hit the streets
men in uniform
love no vinegar
spoon of misery

~~throw give~~ ~~like~~
give a life ~~get a~~ a life
get a lifeline

Citizen Ship

It was nothing. It didn't matter to me
There were tanks all over my city
There was water outside the windows
And children in the streets were throwing rocks at tanks

Ain't got a passport ain't got my real name
Ain't got a chance sport at fortune or fame
As I walk these endless streets won't you give me a lift
A lift a lift on your citizen ship

They were rioting in Chicago movement in L.A.
'68 it broke the Yardbirds. We were broke as well
Took it underground. M.C. borderline. Up against the wall
The wall. The wall. Show your papers boy

Citizen ship we got memories. Stateless they got shame
Cast adrift from the citizen ship lifeline denied exiled this castaway

Blind alley in New York City in a foreign embrace
If you're hungry you're not too particular about what you'll taste
Men in uniform gave me vinegar spoon of misery
But what the hell I fell I fell. It doesn't matter to me

Citizen ship we got memories. Citizen ship we got pain
Cast adrift from the citizen ship lifeline denied exile this castaway

I was caught up like a moth with its wings out of sync
Cut the cord. Overboard. Just a refugee
Lady liberty lend a hand to me I've been cast adrift
Adrift. Adrift. Adrift. Adrift. Adrift. Adrift

On the citizen ship we got memory. Citizen ship we got pain
Lose your grip on the citizen ship you're cast you're cast away
On the citizen ship you got memory. Citizen ship you got pain
Citizen ship you got identity. A name a name a name
A name. Ivan. A name. Ivan Kral. Name. Name.
What's your name son. New York City. What's your name.
What's your name. What's your name. Name. Nothing.
I got nothing. Name. Name. Name. Name. Wake up.
Give me your tired your poor. Give me your huddled masses
Your war torn on your tender seas. Give me your war torn
On your shores of dawn. Lift up your golden lamp to me.
Ahh, it's all mythology

SEVEN WAYS OF GOING

I've got seven ways of going seven wheres to be
Seven sweet disguises, seven ways of serving Thee
Lord, I do extol Thee for Thou hast lifted me
Woke me up and shook me out of mine iniquity
For I was undulating in the lewd impostered night
Steeped in a dream to rend the seams to redeem the rock of right

Swept through the seas of Galilee and the Seven Hills of Rome
Seven sins were wrung from the sight of me
Lord, I turned my neck toward home
I opened up my arms to you and we spun from life to life
'Till you loosened me and let me go toward the everlasting light

In this big step I am taking seven seizures for the true
I got seven ways of going seven ways of serving you
As I move through seven levels as I move upon the slate
As I declare to you the number of my moves as I speculate
The eighth seeking love without exception a light upon the swarm
Seeking love without exception a saint in any form

Nodding though the lamp's lit low. Nod for passers underground
To and fro she's darning and the land is weeping red and pale
Weeping yarn from Algiers. Weeping yarn from Algiers

Weaving though the eyes are pale. What will rend will also mend
The sifting cloth is binding and the dream she weaves will never end
For we're marching toward Algiers. For we're marching toward Algiers

Lullaby though baby's gone. Lullaby a broken song
Oh, the cradle was our call. When it rocked we carried on
And we marched on toward Algiers. Forward marching toward Algiers
We're still marching for Algiers. Marching, marching for Algiers

Not to hail a barren sky. The sifting cloth is weeping red
The mourning veil is waving high a field of stars and tears we've shed
In the sky a broken flag. Children wave and raise their arms
We'll be gone but they'll go on and on and on and on and on

HYMN

When I am troubled in the night
He comes to comfort me

He wills me thru the darkness
And the empty child is free

To take his hand his sacred heart
The heart that breaks the dawn

Amen. And when I think
I've had my fill he fills up again

Time is the space + the wall around
Time to adore and Time to go.
To give to the fisherman
To give up the goes

Time bees the moments
your children will hold
the wave of your hand
the smile of your soul

burning yearning
like some heroine

cara papa

its been a long time since last one
spoke. here is a sad bicycle lying
on its side mourning its wheel.
Which way do we turn. and in turn
when is there to stop turning.
Time is expressed in the heart of
an instrument. Time is the space
and the wall around, ~~sometimes~~.
~~I plead with to the fisherman~~
Time to adore and Time to go
the shoes of the fisherman

Wave

Hi. Hi. I was running after you for a long time. I was watching you for . . . actually I've watched you for a long time. I like to watch you when you're walking back and forth on the beach. And the way your, the way your cloth looks. I like I like to see the edges, the bottom of it get all wet when you're walking near the water there. It's real nice to talk to you. I didn't. I-I-I-I. How are you? How are you? I saw I saw you from your balcony window and you were standing there waving at everybody. It was really great because there was about a billion people there, but when I was waving to you, the way your face was, it was so, the way your face was, it made me feel exactly like we're, it's not that you were just waving to me, but that we were we were waving to each other. Really it was really wonderful. I really felt happy. It really made me happy. And. Um. I. I just wanted to thank you because you, you really really you made me feel good and, oh, I, it's nothing. Well I'm just clumsy. No, it's just a Band-Aid. No, it's OK. Oh no, I'm always doing. Something's always happening to me. Well. I'll be seeing you. Good-bye. Bye. Good-bye sir. Good-bye papa.

Wave thou art pretty, Wave thou art high
Wave thou art music, Wave thou art why
Wave thou art pretty, Wave thou art high
Wave to the city, wave wave good-bye

—*for Albino Luciano, Pope John Paul I*

DREAM OF LIFE

Peace, peace! he is not dead, he doth not sleep—
He hath awakened from the dream of life—

—PERCY BYSSHE SHELLEY

PEOPLE HAVE THE POWER

I was dreaming in my dreaming
Of an aspect bright and fair
And my sleeping it was broken
But my dream it lingered near
In the form of shining valleys
Where the pure air recognized
And my senses newly opened
But I awakened to the cry
That the people have the power
To redeem the work of fools
From the meek the graces shower
It's decreed the people rule

The people have the power
The people have the power

Vengeful aspects became suspect
And bending low as if to hear
And the armies ceased advancing
Because the people had their ear
And the shepherds and the soldiers
Lay beneath the stars
Exchanging visions
Laying arms
To waste in the dust
In the form of shining valleys
Where the pure air recognized
And my senses newly opened
I awakened to the cry

The people have the power
The people have the power

Where there were deserts
I saw fountains
Like cream the waters rise
And we strolled there together
With none to laugh or criticize
And the leopard
And the lamb
Lay together truly bound
I was hoping in my hoping
To recall what I had found
I was dreaming in my dreaming
God knows a purer view
As I surrender to my sleeping
I commit my dream to you

The people have the power
The power to dream to rule
To wrestle the Earth from fools
It's decreed the people rule
It's decreed the people rule
Listen. I believe everything we dream
Can come to pass through our union
We can turn the world around
We can turn the earth's revolution

We have the power
People have the power

UP THERE DOWN THERE

Up there
There's a ball of fire
Some call it the spirit
Some call it the sun
Its energies are not for hire
It serves man it serves everyone
Down there where Jonah wails
In the healing water
In the ready depths
Twisting like silver swans
No line of death no boundaries

Up there
The eye is hollow
The eye is winking
The winds ablaze
Angels howling
The sphinx awakens
But what can she say
You'd be amazed

Down there
Your days are numbered
Nothing to fear
There will be trumpets
There will be silence
In the end the end
Will be here just here

Ahh the borders of heaven
Are zipped up tight tonight
The abstract streets
The lights like some
Switched-on Mondrian
Cats like us are obsolete
Hey Man don't breathe on my feet
Thieves, poets we're inside out
And everybody's a soldier
Angels howl at those abstract lights
And the borders of heaven
Are zipped up tight tonight

Up there
There's a ball of fire
Some call it the spirit
Some call it the sun
Its energies are not for hire
It serves man it serves everyone

The air we breathe
The flame of wisdom
The earth we grind
The beckoning sea
It's no mystery
Not sentimental
Ahh the equation
It's all elemental

The world is restless
Heaven in flux
Angels appear
From the bright storm
Out of the shadows
Up there, down there
But what can we say
Man's been forewarned

All communion is not holy
Even those that fall
They can prophet
Understanding
It's all for man
It's for everyone
It's up there,
Down there
Everywhere
Everywhere
Time for communion
Time for communion
Talking communion

Speak to me
Speak to me heart
I feel a needing
To bridge the clouds
Softly go
A way I wish to know to know
A way I wish to know to know

Oh you'll ride
Surely dance in a ring
Backwards and forwards
Those who seek
Feel the glow
A glow we all will know
A glow we all will know

On that day filled with grace
On the way two hearts' communion
Steps we take steps we trace
On the way two hearts' reunion

Paths that cross
Will cross again
Paths that cross
Will cross again

Speak to me
Speak to me shadow
I spin from the wheel
Nothing at all save the need
The need to weave

A silk of souls
That whisper whisper
A silk of souls
That whispers to me

Speak to me heart
All things renew
Hearts will mend
'Round the bend
Paths that cross
Cross again
Paths that cross
Will cross again

Rise up hold the reins
We'll meet
I don't know when
Hold tight bye bye
Paths that cross
Will cross again
Paths that cross
Will cross again

—for Samuel J. Wagstaff Jr.

SOMALIA

I don't know why I feel this way today
The sky is blue the table is laid
The trees are heavy with yellow fruit
And in their shade children happily play

The pears have fallen to the ground
My child places one in my hand
The sun is warm upon my face
And I dream of a burning land

Mother of famine take this pear
Upon an arrow through the rings of time
This small fruit this golden prayer
May it pass from this hand to thine

If I were rain I'd rain on Somalia
If I were grain for Somalia I'd grow
If I were bread I would rise for Somalia
If I were a river for Somalia I'd flow

All the mothers will dream of thee
All the mothers bless thy empty hand
All the mothers will grieve for thee
All the sorrow a mother can stand

If we were rain we would rain for Somalia
If we were grain for Somalia we'd grow
If we were bread we would rise for Somalia
If we were a river for Somalia we'd flow

—*This lyric was written in memory of Audrey Hepburn, who worked with the simple industry of a servant to give comfort to the victims of the famine in Somalia.*

WILD LEAVES

Wild leaves are falling
Falling to the ground
Every leaf a moment
A light upon the crown
That we'll all be wearing
In a time unbound
And wild leaves are falling
Falling to the ground

Every word that's spoken
Every word decreed
Every spell that's broken
Every golden deed
All the parts we're playing
Binding as the reed
And wild leaves are falling
Wild wild leaves

The spirits that are mentioned
The myths that have been shorn
Everything we've been through
And the colors worn
Every chasm entered
Every story wound
And wild leaves are falling
Falling to the ground

As the campfire's burning
As the fire ignites
All the moments turning
In the stormy bright
Well enough the churning
Well enough believe
The coming and the going
Wild wild leaves

WHERE DUTY CALLS

In a room in Lebanon
They silently slept
They were dreaming
Crazy dreams
In a foreign alphabet
Lucky young boys
Cross on the main
The driver was approaching
The American zone
The waving of hands
The tiniest train
They never dreamed
They'd never wake again

Voice of the Swarm
We follow we fall
Some kneel for priests
Some wail at walls
Flag on a match head
God or the law
And they'll all go together
Where duty calls

United children
Child of Iran
Parallel prayers
Baseball Koran

I'll protect mama
I'll lie awake
I'll die for Allah
In a holy war
I'll be a ranger
I'll guard the streams
I'll be a soldier
A sleeping marine

In the heart of the ancient
Ali smiles
In the soul of the desert
The sun blooms
Awake into the glare
Of all our little wars
Who pray to salute
The coming and dying
Of the moon
Oh sleeping sun

Assassin in prayer
Laid a compass deep
Exploding dawn
And himself as well
Their eyes for his eyes
Their breath for his breath
All to his end

And a room in Lebanon
Dust of scenes
Erase and blend
May the blanket of kings
Cover them and him

Forgive them Father
They know not what they do
From the vast portals
Of their consciousness
They're calling to you

—This lyric was written in memory of those who lost their lives in the destruction of the First Battallion, 8th Marine Headquarters, Beirut, October 23, 1983. Two hundred and forty-one marines, sailors, and soldiers on a peacekeeping mission perished with their assassin.

DREAM OF LIFE

I'm with you always
You're ever on my mind
In a light to last a whole life through
Each way I turn the sense of you surrounds
In every step I take in all I do
Your thoughts your schemes
Captivate my dreams
Everlasting ever new
Sea returns to sea and sky to sky
In a life of dream am I when I'm with you

Deep in my heart
How the presence of you shines
In a light to last a whole life through
I recall the wonder of it all
Each dream of life I'll share with you

I'm with you always
You're ever on my mind
In a light to last a whole life through
The hand above turns those leaves of love
All and all a timeless view
Each dream of life
Flung from paradise
Everlasting ever new
Dream of Life, dream of Life

The Hit Factory inc.

237 West 54th street, New York, N.Y.10019

tel. 664-1000

GOING UNDER

SUN IS RISING
ON THE WATER
LIGHT IS DANCING AGAIN
LETS GO UNDER
WHERE THE SUN BEAMS
LETS GO UNDER
MY FRIEND

ARE WE SLEEPING
ARE WE DREAMING
ARE WE DANCING AGAIN
IS IT HEAVEN
CRACK IT OPEN
AND WE'LL SLIDE DOWN
IT'S STREAM

WE CAN HOLD ON (I'M SURE)
TO THE SEA'S FOAMING MANE
IT WILL SERVE US
WE'LL SURFACE
AND WE'LL PLUNGE BACK AGAIN

SUN IS RISING
ON THE WATER
LIGHT IS DANCING
LIKE A FLAME
THERES NO BURNING
WHERE THE SUN BEAMS
OH ITS SUCH A LOVELY GAME

DOES THE SEA DREAM (I'M SURE)
WE ARE HERE, WE ATTEND
WE ARE BELLS ON THE SHORE
WHERE THE TOLLING SUSPENDS

WHO WILL DECIDE
THE SHAPE OF THINGS
THE SHIFT OF BEING
WHO WILL PERCEIVE
WHEN LIFE IS NEW
SHALL WE DIVIDE
AND BECOME ANOTHER
WHO IS DUE
FOR GIFT UPON GIFT
WHO WILL DECIDE
SHALL WE SWIM/OVER AND OVER
THE CURVE OF A WING
IT'S DESTINATION
EVERCHANGING

SUN IS RISING
ON THE WATER
LIGHT IS DANCING
LIKE A FLAME
LETS GO WALTZING
ON THE WATER
LETS GO UNDER
AGAIN

LETS GO UNDER
~~KEEP~~
going under

GOING UNDER

Sun is rising on the water
Light is dancing again
Let's go under
Where the sun beams
Let's go under my friend

Are we sleeping
Are we dreaming
Are we dancing again
Is it heaven crack it open
And we'll slide down its stream

We can hold on I'm sure
To the sea's foaming mane
It will serve us
We'll surface
And we'll plunge back again

Sun is rising on the water
Light is dancing like a flame
There's no burning
Where the sun beams
Oh it's such a lovely game

Does the sea dream I'm sure
We are here, we attend
We are bells on the shore
As the tolling suspends

Who will decide the shape of things
The shift of being
Who will perceive when life is new
Shall we divide and become another
Who is due for gift upon gift
Who will decide
Shall we swim over and over
The curve of a wing
Its destination ever changing

Sun is rising on the water
Light is dancing like a flame
Let's go waltzing on the water
Let's go under again
Let's go under
Going under

AS THE NIGHT GOES BY

Darlin' come under cover
Another night to discover
Let's slip where senses gather
Let's drift between the sea and sky
As the night goes by

Sands shift
Orchids so strange
In the moonlight
Brushing our faces
Places where love blooms
And dies
While the night goes by
Oh, and the spirits call
Sun upon your shadows fall
Tracing every breath we draw

Come into my dreams
Come into my dreams
Darlin' let's go where the night goes
Let's drift where senses gather
Let's make this night last forever
Into my dreams
Into my dreams

Darlin' let's go
Where the night goes
Time slips
Oh darlin' how it flies
When the night goes by

All through the night
Sirens call
Come to me
I'll come to you
As the night softly
Goes by bye

Midnight
Moon on our shoulder
Daybreak
Another one older
Darlin' heavenly blue
Glories fade into view

Let's go
Under the stars
That are beating
Under the moonlight
Stars shoot
Dusk just a whisper
Make this night
Last forever
Oh how I wonder
Where the night goes
Oh let's wonder
Where the night goes
As the night goes
By bye
By bye

LOOKING FOR YOU (I WAS)

In the medieval night
'Twas love's design
And the sky was open
Like a valentine
All the lacy lights
Where wishes fall
And like Shakespeare's child
I wished on them all

Ahh to be your destiny
Was all that I pursued
I could see the sights
From the lofty heights
But my heart obscured the view

I was looking for you
Looking for you
What could I do
I was looking for you

Along the black river
The ambassador jewels
And you were reflected
In all that I saw
In the towers of gold
In the wheel and the wing
Gripping my senses
Like an ancient claim

Many is the time I knelt in the light
Appealing to all that I knew
Guide my eyes and steps
That I may find love true

I was looking for you
Looking for you
What could I do
I was looking for you

Come on darlin'
All that hearts desire
Was written before us
In the medieval fire
It was love's design
In the glittering stars
Like Shakespeare's child
To be where you are

From the Portobello Road
To the Port of Marseilles
Where the dervish turns
Where the wild goats play

Looking for you
I was

MEMORIAL SONG

Little emerald bird
Wants to fly away
If I cup my hand
Could I make him stay
Little emerald soul
Little emerald eye
Little emerald soul
Must you say good-bye

All the things that we pursue
All that we dream
Are composed as nature knew
In a feather green

Little emerald bird
As you light afar it
is true I heard
God is where you are
Little emerald soul
Little emerald eye
Little emerald bird
We must say good-bye

—for Robert Mapplethorpe

THE JACKSON SONG

Little blue dreamer go to sleep
Let's close our eyes and call the deep
Slumbering land that just begins
When day is done and little dreamers spin

First take my hand then let it go
Little blue boy you're on your own
Little blue wings as those feet fly
Little blue shoes that walk across the sky

May your path be your own
But I'm with you
And each day you'll grow
He'll be there too
And someday you'll go
We'll follow you
As you go, as you go

Little blue star that offers light
Little blue bird that offers flight
Little blue path where those feet fall
Little blue dreamer won't you dream it all

May your path be your own
But I'm with you
And each day you'll grow
He'll be there too
And someday you'll go
We'll follow you
As you go, as you go

And in your travels you will see
Warrior wings remember Daddy
And if a mama bird you see
Folding her wings will you remember me
As you go, as you go, as you go, as you go

GONE AGAIN

———————————

*Thou hast turned for me my mourning
into dancing.*

—PSALM 30:11

What happened afterward you know, precious friend, said the friend, from what was sung and not sung: the birch trees, the little hotel in Paris where Genet died, an elbow, an armpit, too many cigarettes, wigs hung on long poles, the strangers in the little room below, the injured telephone—don't touch. The shaft of light that died in the mud, the slender whirling and swaying, shouting and standing tall. Hic dissonant ubique, nam enim sic diversis cantilenis clamore solent. Here all voices are at variance, as different songs are being roared out simultaneously. The day was still perfect, the children lovable, distracting, and everybody, from the crushed to the exalted, swayed in the music's updraft. Not bored. Not discouraged. Women were sassier, and felt sexier. Because of you, precious friend. The music spread everywhere. In the mouth. In the armpits. In the crotch. The music a way of flying up and flying past. I remember the saliva, and also the slap and the creased newspapers. You left and then you returned. You grinned. Your grin is still irresistible. Take back the night. Take back your life. And chant and squat and jump and shout, *Aux vaincus!* To the conquered!

—Susan Sontag

GONE AGAIN

Hey now man's own kin
We commend into the wind
Grateful arms grateful limbs
Grateful soul he's gone again

I have a winter's tale
How vagrant hearts relent prevail
Sow their seed into the wind
Seize the sky and they're gone again

Fame is fleeting god is nigh
We raise our arms to him on high
We shoot our flint into the sun
We bless our spoils and we're gone we're gone

Hey now man's own kin
We commend into the wind
Grateful arms grateful limbs
Grateful heart he's gone again

Here a man, man's own kin
Turned his back and his own people shot him
And he fell on his knees
Before the burning plain
And he beheld fields of gold his land his son
And he arose his blood aflame
Clouds pressed with hand prints stained

One last breath
The sky is high
The hungry earth
The empty vein

The ashes rain
Death's own bed
Man's own kin
Into the wind
One last breath
Hole in life
Love knot tied
Braid undone
A child born
The hollow horn
A warrior cried
A warrior died
One last breath
Lick of flame
Spirit moaned
Spirit shed
The heavens fed
Man's own kin
Grips the sky
And he's gone again

Hey now man's own kin
We lay down into the wind
Grateful arms grateful limbs
Grateful heart is gone again

Hey now man's own kin
He ascends into the wind
Grateful arms grateful limbs
Grateful man he's gone again

BENEATH THE SOUTHERN CROSS

Oh
To be
Not
Anyone
Gone
This maze
Of being
Skin
Oh to cry
Not any cry
So mournful
That
The dove
Just laughs
And
The steadfast
Gasps
Oh to owe
Not anyone
Nothing
To be
Not here
But here
Forsaking
Equatorial bliss
Who walked
Through
The callow mist
Dressed in scraps

Who walked
The curve
Of the world
Whose bone
Scraped
Whose flesh
Unfurled
Who grieves
Not
Anyone gone
To greet lame
The inspired sky
Amazed to stumble
Where gods
Get lost
Beneath
The southern
Cross

—*for Oliver Ray*

Oh
To be
not
anyone
gone
The
maze
of being
skin / o LIVE OR
ungainly limbs
will
walk on
steadfast
stuff
mercurial
detached

who grieves not
being
gone.

Tossed.

oh
To be
not
anyone
expecting
X
pelling
cries
so mournful
The
dove
just
laughs
and
The

just
gasps.

Confounding
every
pilgrim
sailor
anyone
imprisoned
in
their
net of skin

oh
To owe
nothing
anyone
To be too
hot
here
but
here
dressed
in scraps
into smoke
Equatorial
blaze
who walks
thru
the
calloused
mists
who
walked
The curve
of the arms
whose
to
flesh
unfurled
who
grieves
not
the

where gods get
lost

points
To
nothing
anyone
gone

until
you
flesh
unfurled
waving
beneath
these
line
points.

Saint
breath
the
Southern
Cross

Beneath the Southern Cross

Toward another he has gone
To breathe an air beyond his own
Toward a wisdom beyond the shelf
Toward a dream that dreams itself
About a boy beyond it all
About a boy beyond it all

From the forest from the foam
From the field that he had known
Toward a river twice as blessed
Toward the inn of happiness
About a boy beyond it all
About a boy beyond it all

From a chaos raging sweet
From the deep and dismal street
Toward another kind of peace
Toward the great emptiness
About a boy beyond it all
About a boy beyond it all

I stood among them I listened
I stood among them I listened not
I stood among them and I heard myself
Who I've loved better than you
So much so that I walked on
Into the face of God
Away from your world
And my sour stomach
Into the face of God, who said
Boy, I knew thee not, but boy
Now that I have you in my face
I embrace you. I welcome you
He was just a boy
Whirling in the snow
Just a little boy
Who would never grow

—for Kurt Cobain

MY MADRIGAL

We waltzed beneath motionless skies
All heaven's glory turned in your eyes
We expressed such sweet vows

Oh 'till death do us part
Oh 'till death do us part

We waltzed beneath God's point of view
Knowing no ending to our rendezvous
We expressed such sweet vows

Oh 'till death do us part
Oh 'till death do us part

We waltzed beneath motionless skies
All heaven's glory turned in your eyes
You pledged me your heart
'Till death do us part
You pledged me your heart
'Till death do us part

'Till death do us part

SUMMER CANNIBALS

I was down in Georgia
Nothing was as real
As the street beneath my feet
Descending into air

The cauldron was a'bubbling
The flesh was lean
And the women moved forward
Like piranhas in a stream
They spread themselves before me
An offering so sweet
And they beckoned
And they beckoned
Come on darling eat

Eat the summer cannibals
Eat Eat Eat
You eat the summer cannibals
Eat Eat Eat

They circled around me
Natives in a ring
And I saw their souls a'withering
Like snakes in chains
And they wrapped themselves around me
Ummm what a treat
And they rattled their tales
hissing come on let's eat

Eat the summer cannibals
Eat Eat Eat
You eat the summer cannibals
Eat Eat Eat

I felt a rising in my throat
The girls a'saying grace
And the air, the vicious air
Pressed against my face
And it all got too damn much for me
Just got too damn rough
And I pushed away my plate
And said boys I've had enough
And I laid upon the table
Just another piece of meat
And I opened up my veins to them
And said come on eat

Eat the summer cannibals
Eat Eat Eat
You eat the summer cannibals
Eat Eat Eat

'Cause I was down in Georgia
Nothing was as real
As the street beneath my feet
Descending into hell
So Eat Eat Eat
Eat Eat Eat

DEAD TO THE WORLD

Dead to the world my body was sleeping
On my mind was nothing at all
Come a mist an air so appealing
I'm here a whisper you summoned I called

I formed me a presence whose aspect was changing
Oh he would shift he would not shift at all
We sat for a while he was very engaging
And when he was gone I was gone on a smile

With a strange way of walking
And a strange way of breathing
More lives than a cat
That led me astray
All in all he captured my heart
Dead to the world and I just
Slipped away

I heard me a music that drew me to dancing
Lo I turned under his spell
I opened my coat but he never came closer
I bolted the door and I whispered oh well

I laid in the rushes the air was upon me
Wondering well I just couldn't discern
Will he come back come back to me
Oh I whispered will you ever return

I was feeling sensations in no dictionary
He was less than a breath of shimmer and smoke
The life in his fingers unwound my existence
Dead to the world alive I awoke

With a strange way of walking
And a strange way of breathing
Less than a breath of shimmer and smoke
The life in his fingers unwound my existence
Dead to the world alive I awoke

dead to the world

F/m

1st

2nd   Then lft this
        one

3rd

weird chord

1st

2nd

an F
with this

I was feeling sensations
in no dictionary
I opened my coat.
but he never came close
he was less than
    a whisper
of shimmer and smoke
the life in his fingers
unwound my existance
dead to the world
alive il awoke

Spectral Dance

Dead to the World

Ravens

Common favors seek us all   D
and slip our binding rings   A
will turn our necks
And make us reel   D
will bear our arms   A
as wings
Above the crown
a feather drifts   F
before us it will fall   A
for Time will hail   D
and bid us rise   A
make ravens of us all

My love to breathe
The air of Kings
Yet fell beneath his luck
Within his heart a yearning yet
before his Time Time shook
All the gifts that god had taxed F male   (and those that fate denighed)
and those by labors high
returned to where all treasure made laid
And where The ravens fly

                                  e agree
There are places yet to be
Where is yet to roam
The Egyptian Plain
The artic sea
Where shadows draw me on
No where but sky it have to go
                          the
When I return to thee
                              me
but for a time Time has spared

Til I a raven be

                        For me Time Time has
                            spared

Ravens, 1996

RAVENS

Common fortune seeks us all
And slips our binding rings
We'll turn our heads
And make us reel
We'll bare our arms as wings
Before our feet a feather drifts
Beyond us it will fall
'Cause time will bid and make us rise
Make ravens of us all

My love he breathed the air of kings
Yet fell beneath his luck
And in his heart a yearning yet
Before his time time shook
And all the gifts that god had gave
And those by fate denied
Gone to where all treasures laid
And where the raven flies

Oh there are places I agree
Where I have yet to roam
The Egyptian field the arctic sea
Where shadows haunt and moan
But none but sky I have to go
Should I return to thee
Gone to where the feather flies
'Till I a raven be

I been a'walking
Wherefore am I walking
I been a'walking
If you see me walking
A'walking a'wandering
If you see me walking
Don't ever turn your eye
Don't turn away don't turn away
I'm coming to you
Eleven steps 'till I can rest
Eleven steps 'till I'm blessed by you

I and I alone can but do for you
To twist in my hand the thorn of thy youth
To draw thy seed to turn in birth
Thy sighs thy moans I and I alone

Nine steps 'till I can rest
Nine steps 'till I'm blessed by you
I will wash your feet and dry them with my hair
I will give to you every other tear
Thy mouth thy spear thy season of mirth
Seven steps until I can rest
Seven steps 'till I'm blessed by you

All I ever wanted I wanted I wanted
All I ever wanted I wanted from you
Thy highs thy lows I and I alone
Ghost of thy ghost walk I will walk
A burning stem to illume thy night
Five steps 'till I can rest

Five steps 'till I'm blessed by you
Four steps until I can rest
Four steps 'till I'm blessed by you
Three steps until I get to you
Two steps until I can rest
Two steps 'till I'm blessed by you
Blood of my blood bone of my bone
Can but do for you I and I alone

FAREWELL REEL

It's been a hard time
And when it rains
It rains on me
The sky just opens
And when it rains
It pours

I walk alone
Assaulted it seems
By tears of heaven
And darling I can't help
Thinking those tears are yours

Our wild love came from above
And wilder still
Is the wind that howls
Like a voice that knows it's gone
'Cause darling you died
And well I cried
But I'll get by
Salute our love
And send you a smile
And move on

So darling farewell
All will be well
And then all will be fine
The children will rise
Strong and happy be sure
'Cause your love flows
And the corn still grows

And God only knows
We're only given
As much as the heart can endure

But I don't know why
But when it rains
It rains on me
The sky just opens
And when it rains
It pours

But I look up
And a rainbow appears
Like a smile from heaven
And darling I can't
Help thinking that smile
Is yours

COME BACK LITTLE SHEBA

Come back little Sheba
I hear them calling
Open your eyes
Awake from thy sleep

High above
The stars are falling
Open your arms
And you shall receive

The lights of the city
So bold and flashing
All of its riches
Imparted to thee

Robes of saffron
Robes of standing
A road of crimson
Spread at your feet

Your robes of standing
Your robes of saffron
Your road of crimson
All pleasing to me

But close your lights
Close your gates
I must arise
My flock awaits

Farewell little Sheba
I hear them a'calling
Here is your staff
Tend to thy sheep

Good wishes be with you
If that be your calling
Farewell little Sheba
Arise and take leave

WING

I was a wing in heaven blue
Soared over the ocean
Soared over Spain
And I was free
Needed nobody
It was beautiful

I was a pawn
Didn't have a move
Didn't have nowhere
That I could go
But I was free
I needed nobody
It was beautiful
It was beautiful

I was a vision
In another eye
And they saw nothing
No future at all
Yet I was free
I needed nobody
It was beautiful
It was beautiful

And if there's one thing
Could do for you
You'd be a wing
In heaven blue

PEACE AND NOISE

Through the empty arch comes a wind, a mental wind blowing relentlessly over the heads of the dead, in search of new landscapes and unknown accents . . . announcing the constant baptism of newly created things.

—FEDERICO GARCÍA LORCA, *IN SEARCH OF DUENDE*

WAITING UNDERGROUND

If you believe all your hope is gone
Down the drain of your humankind
The time has arrived
You be waiting here
As I was in a snow white shroud
Waiting underground

There by the ridge, be a gathering
Beneath the pilgrim moon
Where we shall await, the beat
Of your feet, hammering the earth
Where the great ones tremble
In their snow white shrouds
Waiting underground

If you seek the kingdom, come along
Waiting by the ridge, be a gathering
Beneath the pilgrim moon
Where the river thunders
There we shall await, the beat
Of your feet, hammering the earth
And as the earth resounds
And humankind becomes as one
Then we will arise to be as one

But until that day we will just await
In our snow white shrouds
Waiting underground
Waiting underground

Hello friend I've come a'calling
Passively stationed active patrol
Sliding in high noon
Like some reluctant sheriff
Not want to get involved in it all
Who stands guard for each other
Why must we guard anything at all
Anything at all

From the earth's four corners the people are calling
Forming equations but the questions are hard
All men are brothers killing each other
And mother earth is wringing in wonder
Who stands guard for each other
Why must we guard anything at all.
Anything at all
Whirl away now
Whirl away now
Whirl away

There's a cross on the road, there's a great mill turning
Some seeking answers, some are born with answers
You can hold on the blade and turn around forever
Be flung into space into another kind of grace
Who stands guard for each other
Why must we guard anything at all.
Anything at all
Whirl away now
Whirl away now
Whirl away

Some give of the hand
Some give of their land
Some giveth their life
Laying in a field of grain
The staff of life all around you
Yet you will cut someone down
For their possessions

Some material thing
And our children are being blown away
Like wishes in the wind
For the sake of their coat
Or their colors or their code
Or the color of their skin
Or the name of their shoes
And the mother cries why'd they take my son
And the father wonders why'd they take my boy
He extended his hand he gave of his land
He gave of his bread he gave of his heart
Said hello friend
Hello friend
Hello friend
Hello friend

1959

Listen to my story
Got two tales to tell
One of fallen glory
One of vanity
The world's roof was raging
We were looking fine
'Cause we built that thing
And it grew wings
In 1959

Wisdom was a teapot, pouring from above
Desolation angels served it up with love
Igniting life every form of light
Moved by bold design
Slid in that thing
And it grew wings
In 1959

It was blue and shining in the sun
Braced, native
Speeding the American plain
Into freedom freedom freedom

China was a tempest
And madness overflowed
The lama was a young man
And watched his world in flames
Taking glory down
By the edge of clouds
It was a crying shame

Another lost horizon
Tibet the fallen star
Wisdom and compassion crushed
In the land of Shangri-la
But in the land of the Impala honey
Well we were looking fine
'Cause we built that thing and it grew wings in 1959
'Cause we built that thing and it grew wings in 1959
'Cause we built that thing and it grew wings in 1959

It was the best of times, it was the worst of times in 1959
It was the best of times, it was the worst of times in 1959

BLUE POLES

Mother as I write the sun dissolves
Blood life streaming cross my hand
And these words, these words
Hope dashed immortal hope
Hope streaking the canvas sky
Blue poles infinitely winding, as I write, as I write
Blue poles infinitely winding, as I write, as I write

We joined the long caravan
Hungry dreaming going west
Just for work just to get a job
And we never got lucky
We just forged on
And the dust the endless dust
Like a plague it covered everything
Hal fell with the fever
And mother I did what I could
Blue poles infinitely winding, as I write, as I write
Blue poles infinitely winding, as I write, as I write

We prayed we prayed for rain
I never wanted to see the sun again

All my dresses you made by hand
We left behind on the road
Hal died in my arms
We buried him by the river
Blue poles infinitely winding, as I write, as I write
Blue poles infinitely winding, as I write, I write

DON'T SAY NOTHING

Lower the thing the skin of a cat
Skin it to the left just laying there
No other thing is luck like that
And you set it said it said nothing

Went to the party very discouraged
I watched the litter pile like a wall
I looked at the river just couldn't forgive it
It was ladened with all kinds of shit
Still I admit that I didn't say nothing
I turned my back walked away
Got to face the fact that I didn't say nothing

Everyone was dancing I stood over in the corner
I was listening they were saying this and saying that
And putting this one down but nothing was delivered
Nothing good was coming I just stood there
I couldn't believe it but I didn't say nothing
I walked the floor then I looked away
Got to face the fact that I didn't say nothing

How long how long will we make do
Maybe it's time to break on through
Gonna lift my skirts gonna straighten up
Gonna get well I'm gonna do something
Gonna face the fact gonna pay it back
And I'm gonna do something won't hold my tongue
Won't hold the thought won't hold the card
Well I'm gonna do something
Oh my brain I got to complain

You can refrain but I'm gonna do something
How long how long will we make do
Maybe it's time to break on through

Out in the desert I saw that old cat skinned
I saw it floating in the river
I saw and no one seemed to mind
They sat there they sat there watching the sun
I saw it float away and I watched the buildings crumble
Like dust in the hand and we watched the sun
Spread its wings and fly away
And in the mountains a cry echoes
Don't say nothing
Don't say nothing no
Don't say nothing no

DEAD CITY

This dead city longs to be
This dead city longs to be free
Seven screaming horses
Melt down in the sun
Building scenes on empty dreams
And smoking them one by one

This dead city longs to be
This dead city longs to be living
Is it any wonder there's squalor in the sun
With their broken schemes and their lotteries
They never get nowhere

Is it any wonder they're spitting at the sun
God's parasites in abandoned sites
And they never have much fun

If I was a blind man
Would you see for me
Or would you confuse
The nature of my blues
And refuse a hand to me

Is it any wonder crying in the sun
Is it any wonder I'm crying in the sun
Well I built my dreams on your empty scenes
Now I'm burning them one by one

This damn city this dead city
Immortal city
Motor city
Suc-cess city
Longs to be
Longs to be
Free
Free
Free

DEATH SINGING

In the straw-colored light
In light rapidly changing
On a life rapidly fading

Have you seen death singing
Have you seen death singing

With a throat smooth as a lamb
Yet dry as a branch not snapping
He throws back his head
And he does not sing a thing mournful

Have you seen death singing
Have you seen death singing
Have you seen death singing
In the straw-colored light

He sings a black embrace
And white opals swimming
In a child's leather purse
Have you seen death swimming
Have you seen death swimming

With a throat smooth as a lamb
Yet dry as a branch not snapping
He throws back his head
And he does not sing a thing mournful

Have you seen death singing
Have you seen death singing
Have you seen death singing
In the straw-colored light

He sings of youth enraged
And the burning of Atlanta
And these viral times
And May ribbons streaming
And straw-colored curls a'turning
A mother's vain delight
And woe to the sun
And woe to the dawn
And woe to the young
Another hearse is drawn
Have you seen death singing
In the straw-colored light

—*for Benjamin Smoke*

having spun so
many prayers
That recede as you
sleep and memory
enhabits your dreams
Radiant ones when
the Trials of a
people were
radiant Trials
when the
egg
of
deceptions
egg
cracks
and
they

Its time to go
That we have to go
attain is suddenly
elusive and way
its Time
to go
by
to
Eve

Memento Mori

The fan whirling like the blades of a copter
Lifting into the skies above a foreign land
Fire and iron soaked with the bodies of so many friends
Johnny waved. He was on his way home
He waved good-bye to his comrades in arms
And all the twisted things he had seen
He waved good-bye
And the blades hit something
Maybe just fate but the blades hit
The copter went up in flames
And Johnny never went marching home
And Johnny never went marching home
They took his name and they carved it on a slab of marble
With several thousand other names
All the fallen idols
The apples of their mother's eye
Just another name

Meanwhile back on that burning shore
Johnny's comrades stood speechless
They looked up up up with misbelieving eyes
'Cause there were bits of metal and the embers
The embers of his eyes fanned out in the air
Black dust flames. Oh Johnny
Someday they'll make a movie about you
And in the making of that movie, some mad apocalypse
It will become even stranger than the simple act
Just a boy going up. Up. Up
Just a boy going up. Up. Up

In flames in the smoke
Just another life
Just another breath
And who'll remember
Oh eternity now
As eternal as a sheet of marble
Eternal as a slab

On a green hill
And your name
And all your fallen brothers
And all the ones not cut
All the ones remembered
Only in the hearts
A mother a father a brother
A sister a lover son daughter
Young man shall not fade shall not fade
Your ancestors salute you greet you
And the gods of your ancestors salute you
Having been formed by the mind of your ancestors
The gods of your ancestors salute you
Having been formed by your ancestors
The gods of your ancestors salute you
They draw you in
They draw you through
They draw they draw you
Through that golden door
Come on in boy
We remember you
We conceived you
We conceived of your breath

We conceived of the whole human race
And we conceived it to be a beautiful thing
Like a tulip bending in the wind
Sometimes it comes back to us
In the form of the hand filled with dust
Comes back in the form of a smitten child
Our raped daughters
The broken bones
Souls cleaved of hearts
They come back to us

Our hands are filled
With their rotting tissues
But we turn not our backs
We press our lips
Into their cancer
Into the dust
Into the remains of each one
And that love is there
And will greet you
Come on in boy
It's eternal love

Well here go ahead
Run through that plane
Oh man running through your mind
You took a cat
You took a life
You took it by the tail
And you swirled it around your head
And you thrashed it

You smashed the life out of it
Then you knew that would be your own
But you wanted to feel the dying
Because you knew
You would feel your own
You would feel your own
But you're remembered
You're remembered
You're remembered good
We remember
We remember
We remember
Everything

—*for James Folvary*

LAST CALL

In a mansion high the young man stood
Ready to join his companions good
Outside the scent of magnolia blossoms
Down streets of gold the children were racing

Just another wandering soul
Adrift among the stars
Just another human heart
Led, led away

He put his shoes on and he laid down
Outside the clouds were swiftly gathering
He drained his cup and he stirred the mixture
And he closed his eyes as his conscience whispered

Just another wandering soul
Adrift among the stars
Just another human heart
Led, led away

Misgivings unspoken he joined his companions
His face covered over in a mansion high
Outside the children gazed in wonder
At the quickening sky then slowly disbanded

Thirty-nine wandering souls
Adrift among the stars
Thirty-nine human hearts
Led, led away

Last Call

In a mansion high the young man stood
ready to join his companions good
outside the scent of magnolia blossoms
down streets of gold the children were racing

He put his shoes on and he lay down
~~outside the clouds furiously gathered~~
he drained the cup he stirred the mixture
he closed his eyes as his conscience whispered

outside the clouds furiously gathered
outside the moon vaguely racing
outside the children gazing in wonder
~~at the thund~~

outside the moon vaguely racing
~~outside the clouds furiously gather~~
        watching
stirred by   outside the children

        echoing laughter

Last Call

His burning skin cooled by angels
Swallowing sorrows excretion
It's all excretion
Felled by his hand
Or the mind of another man
Who makes the decisions
Lends no provisions for mere eternal rides
Learning of course every alien force

Even Christ yearns to be
To possess the skin
And bone the blood of man
Who tends the flock
Who breaks the bread
Who makes his own choices
Won't listen to voices
Accept no false teachers
False preachers, good deeders
With their hands out stretched
To be filled with your money
Your flesh, your breath
Your imagination
Sympathy, empathy
Acknowledge all man
As fellow creation
But don't follow him
Don't be led away

GUNG HO

---

by this merit
may all obtain omniscience
may it defeat the enemy, wrongdoing
from the stormy waves of birth, old age,
*   sickness and death*
from the ocean of samsara may we free all
*   beings*

—BUDDHIST PRAYER DEDICATING
THE MERIT OF ACTION

ONE VOICE

In the garden of consciousness
In fertile mind there lies the dormant seed
Blooming into charity
Conscience breathes a sigh of relief
The confessions of sleep
The awakening seed
Moved by love to serve
We celebrate all merit in life
Ah the confessions of sleep
Unfolding peace
As we extend
According to need
And you will heed the call
All action great and small
Received joyfully
Heaven abounds
Let love resound
If he be mute
Give him a bell
If he be blind an eye
If he be down a hand
Lift up your voice
Lift up your voice
Lift up your voice
Give of your mind one mind
Give of your heart one heart
Give of your voice
One voice

LO AND BEHOLDEN

I was alone and
content in my world
dancing on air
you sent to me
a message that said
I like your style
will you come
to the temple tonight
and dance for me there
I pledge to you
all that you wish
the moon and the stars

Lo and beholden
why don't you give it up
lo and beholden
come on you know it's true
lo and beholden
oh I'm beholden to you

In the palace
there was wild reverie
and the look
in your eyes
as I dropped
veil after veil
was drunken desire
the dove calls
God he notes all
the naked truth

here is my seventh veil and last
it will cost you

The royal word it has been passed
the prophet's head is all I ask
for beauty and the naked truth
it will cost you

Lo and beholden
why don't you give it up
lo and beholden
come on you know it's true
lo and beholden
oh I'm beholden to you

UPRIGHT COME

Hail brother
the distant thunder
is nothing but hearts
beating as one
dance of a million
on God's pavilion
come come
beat on your drum

Awake people arise
awake upright come
fortune is falling like
tears from the skies
open your eyes

Hail sister
won't you come over
to shape reshape
things to come
bow your head
raise your lantern
come come
beat on your drum

United action
is what we need
time to say
everything is going to be
wasted icons wasted lives
like war obsolete

These are the times
the times of our own
these are the shapes
the world we formed
swift is the arrow
dark is the thorn
the slate is clean
the future awaits

Awake

I AM THE BODY
I am the stream
I am the wake
of Everything
They bring me flowers That are MYSELF
GARLANDS OF Blood
That are Myself
They SLAY The Lamb
That is myself
a Praying for The lamb
That is HIMSELF
I am HIM

TORN REBORN
The Cries of our dismay
is Nothing To the wind
BUT Who's To ~~don't~~ ~~who's~~ MIND
kings are lifted up
and kings are thrown
lost RECIEVED RETRIEVED
The Human Tide

BLOODY Human TIDE

Boy Cried Wolf

BOY CRIED WOLF

Oh the story's told been told retold
from the sacred scriptures to the tabloids
all the fuss and fight none above a whisper
from the soul of gold to the belly of a boy

Well they drew him from the forest
like they draw blood
tied him to a tree like St. Sebastian
and he turned his head
and let the arrows fly
through the trees the trees
the ornamental leaves
Boy cried wolf
wolf don't come
wolf within boy cried wolf

In the ancient mold
where they're dancing down
calling to the moon
but it don't answer
and they fell on their knees
and passed the bowl around
and the blood the blood
the sacramental blood
Boy cried wolf
wolf don't come
wolf within boy cried wolf

I am the body I am the stream
I am the wake of everything
they bring me flowers that are myself
garlands of blood that are myself
slain the lamb that is himself

I don't care I don't mind
I don't know
I don't care I don't mind
I don't know

Torn reborn the cries of our dismay
are nothing to the wind
but whose to mind
kings are lifted up
and kings are thrown
lost received retrieved
the human tide

Innocence had its day
Innocence had its day
Innocence innocence

PERSUASION

What is the system that gets around
recruits hearts with its timeless rhythm
the young glow but old men know
it's all a part of some crazy schism

Coming on like the dawn unrelenting light
streets thick with its radiating
it's all aglow but we all know
true love is so complicated

Feeling funny don't know why
on a plane circling high
equation persuasion
it's just persuasion

What is the body that has nobody
go through life with nobody at all
it come and go where the wind blow
when persuasion come to call

Got me reeling don't know why
I'm on a plane circling high
equation persuasion
got the feeling I'm running in place
caught in the orbit of the human race
equation persuasion
it's just persuasion
it's just persuasion
it's just persuasion

What is the body that has nobody
what is the rise without the fall
what is illusion without beauty
what is the system that's no system at all

Hey scout there's no equation
you can't prepare for the heart's invasion
you can't prepare for the heart's invasion
love is its own persuasion

GONE PIE

Hey there
come and take a walk with me
stroll into infinity
we'll stroll along
until the dawn is gone
midnight take it to the twilight
just a little slice of light
let's turn it off and on off and on

Strolling ain't it wonderful
into a light that lingers
on and on, on and on

Strolling ain't it wonderful
stars fall for we two
bathed in a light of our own

Oh life
much too great to sacrifice
come and have another slice
ah life goes on and on

Oh life
may you live a long life
may you live a long life
may you live a long life

CHINA BIRD

One fine day
these words I pray
will breathe a truth
within yourself
upon a shelf
a life anew
so many roads
it's hard to know
what to do
all your dreams
all it seems
is as you choose
for destiny
my china bird
is calling for you

The world turns
the flame burns
bright and true
near and far
where you are
guiding you china bird
the open skies
are yearning for you

If they say
it's not that way
hold your view
and with my love
fly above
alight anew
spread your wings
the open sky
is calling to you
china bird my heart
is yearning for you

If you fly away
I'll be waiting
come what may
all my love a fragile ray
for you for you

—*in memory of Grant H. Smith*

GLITTER IN THEIR EYES

It's been a while since I've seen your face
it's been a while since I've walked this place
I see the monkeys riding on their bikes
racing through the impossible night

You say you're feeling like a new tree
man they'll cut you from limb to limb
pick your pocket with such delight
shake it to the right
shake it in the light

Oh can't you see the glitter
the glitter in their eyes
oh can't you see the glitter
the glitter in their eyes

Genius stalking in new shoes
have you got WTO blues
dust of diamonds
making you sneeze
kids on rollers ready for
running through the junkyards
breezing through the halls
racing through the malls
walking through the walls
they'll strip your mind
just for fun
quoth the raven
yum yum yum

Oh can't you see the glitter
the glitter in their eyes
oh can't you see the glitter
the glitter in their eyes

Children children everywhere
selling souls for souvenirs
sold them out like as not
just for chunks of Ankgor Wat

They'll trade you up
trade you down
your body a commodity
our sacred stage
has been defaced
replaced to grace
the marketplace
Dow is Jonesing at the bit
42nd Disney Street
ragged hearts unraveling
look out kids
the gleam the gleam
all that glitters
is not all that glitters
is not all that glitters

Strange Messengers

I looked upon The book of life
Tracing the lines of face after face
looking down at their naked feet
bound in chains bound in chains
chains of leather chains of gold
Men Knew it was wrong
but They looked away
and paraded them down The colonial streets
and thats how They became ENSLAVED

Those who
have
marched
in Civil
Strife

march again
don't Turn away
The chains
That bound

They came accross in The great ships
Mothers separated from their babes
Husbands standing on The Auction Block
    Bound in chains Bound in chains
    Sold To the plantations To Toil
    in fields of white / White Fields /
    Men Knew it was wrong but they looked away
    and they paraded down The colonial streets
    and Turned their neck Toward a bitter landscape

India
Jefferson

history sends us such strange messengers
They come accross Time
their arms are laid
with even stranger feet
and They swung from ropes

Turner/Brown
garrison
Tubman
Sojo

The lilacs in the
        court yard

Strange Messengers

STRANGE MESSENGERS

I looked upon the book of life
tracing the lines of face after face
looking down at their naked feet
bound in chains bound in chains
chains of leather chains of gold

Men knew it was wrong but we looked away
and paraded them down the colonial streets
and that's how they became enslaved

They came across on the great ships
mothers separated from their babes
husbands standing on the auction block
bound in chains bound in chains
chains of leather chains of gold

Men knew it was wrong but they looked away
and led them to toil in fields of white
as they turned their necks to a bitter landscape

Oh the people I hear them calling
Am I not a man and a brother
Am I not a woman and a sister
we will be heard we will be heard

History sends us such strange messengers
they come down through time
to embrace to enrage
and in their arms even stranger fruit
and they swing from the trees
with their vision in flames
ropes of leather ropes of gold
men knew it was wrong
but they looked away
messengers swinging
from twisted rope
as they turned their necks
to a bitter landscape

GRATEFUL

Ours is just another skin
that simply slips away
you can rise above it
it will shed easily

Like a ship in a bottle
held up to the sun
sails ain't going nowhere
you can count every one
until it crashes unto the earth
and simply slips away
you can hide in the open
or just disappear

Ours is just a craving
and a twist of the wrist
will undo the stopper
with abrupt tenderness
die little sparrow
and awake singing

It all will come out fine
I've learned it line by line
one common wire
one silver thread
all that you desire
rolls on ahead

—*for Jerry Garcia*

NEW PARTY

You say hey
the state of the you-you union
is fine fine fine
I got the feeling that you're lying
I think we need
a new party

They say to me
they say what's the word
I say it's thunderbird
why don't you
fly fly fly
fly away hey
and while you're at it
why don't you
fertilize my lawn
with what's running
from your mouth
hey listen here

We got to get off
our ass or get burned
the worlds troubles
are a global concern
does your child have
fresh water to drink
wherever you are
wherever you are you're invited
to think about this

You say hey
the state of the union
is fine fine fine
I got the feeling that
you're lying lying
think we're gonna need
a new party

When in the course
of human events
it becomes necessary
to take things in your own hands
to take the water from the well
and declare it tainted by greed
we got to surely clean it up
clean our house
our inner house
our outer house
and hey by the way
the human event
is the party of the century
and you're all invited
it's where you are
wherever you are
'cause this party
is for everyone
and the price of admission
is love one another
love brother

LIBBIE'S SONG

If it wasn't for your golden hair
I would not be belonely
if it wasn't for your golden hair
I would not be alone

If it wasn't for your piercing stare
I would not be belonely
if it wasn't for your piercing stare
I would not be alone

I would not waltz in a widow's line
danced in black by God's design
what was yours would not be mine
if it wasn't for your golden hair
I would not be alone

You courted me with princely airs
said you'd love me only
kiss the ribbons in my hair
said darling come and fly

Flower of the Calvary
you swept me off my saddle
lifted me into your life
a soldier's wife was I

You proudly marched to the horn
I prayed for your swift return
I waited for you so forlorn
'Ere to be alone

I longed for you, I longed to die
I was so belonely
the pillow's bare by my side
and yet I shall abide

For heaven has aset for me
companion for eternity
so kiss the ribbons in my hair
say darling come and fly

If it wasn't for your golden hair
I would not be alonely
if it wasn't for your golden hair
I would not be alone

—*for Libbie Custer*

GUNG HO

On a field of red one gold star
raised above his head
raised above his head
he was not like any other
he was just like any other
and the song they bled
was a hymn to him

Awake my little one
the seed of revolution
sewn in the sleeve
of cloth humbly worn
where others are adorned

Above the northern plain
the great birds fly
with great wings
over the paddy fields
and the people kneel
and the men they toil
yet not for their own
and the children are hungry
and the wheel groans

There before the grass hut
a young boy stood
his mother lay dead
his sisters cried for bread
and within his young heart

the seed of revolution sewn
in cloth humbly worn
while others are adorned

And he grew into a man
not like any other
just like any other
one small man
a beard the color of rice
a face the color of tea
who shared the misery
of other men in chains
with shackles on his feet
escaped the guillotine

Who fought against
colonialism imperialism
who remained awake
when others did not
who penned like Jefferson
let independence ring
and the cart of justice turns
slow and bitterly
and the people were crying
plant that seed that seed
and they crawled on their bellies
beneath the great beast
and filled the carts with bodies
where once had been their crops

And the great birds swarm
spread their wings overhead
and his mother dead
and the typhoons and the rain
the jungles in flames
and the orange sun

None could be more beautiful
than Vietnam
nothing was more beautiful
than Vietnam
And his heart stopped beating
and the wheel kept turning
and the words he bled
were a hymn to them
I have served the whole people
I have served my whole country
and as I leave this world
may you suffer union
and my great affection
limitless as sky
filled with golden stars

The question is raised
raised above his head
was he of his word
was he a good man
for his image
fills the southern heart

with none but bitterness
And the people keep crying
and the men keep dying
and it's so beautiful
so beautiful
give me one more turn
give me one more turn
one more turn of the wheel
One more revolution
One more turn of the wheel

—*for Ho Chi Minh*

TRAMPIN'

I'm trampin' trampin'
Try'n-a make heaven my home
I'm trampin' trampin'
Try'n-a make heaven my home
I'm trampin' trampin'
I've never been to heaven
But I've been told
Try'n-a make heaven my home
That the streets up there
Are paved with gold
Try'n-a make heaven my home

—EDWARD BOATNER

PATTI SMITH
Bowery Ballroom
December 30   December 31   2000

Patti Smith   Oliver Ray   Jay Dee Daugherty
Lenny Kaye   Tony Shanahan

"AND WHAT SHOULDER AND WHAT ART
COULD TWIST THE SINEWS OF THY HEART"

W.B.

JUBILEE

Oh glad day to celebrate
'Neath the cloudless sky
Air so sweet
Water pure
Fields ripe with rye
Come one, come all
Gather 'round
Discard your Sunday shoes
Come on now
Oh my land
Be a jubilee
Come on girl
Come on boy
Be a jubilee

Oh my land
Oh my good
People don't be shy
Weave the birth of harmony
With children's happy cries
Hand in hand
We're dancing 'round
In a freedom ring
Come on now
Oh my land
Be a jubilee
Come on girl
Come on boy
Be a jubilee

We will never fade away
Doves shall multiply
Yet I see hawks circling the sky
Scattering our glad day
With debt and despair
What good hour
Will restore our troubled air?
Come on people
Gather 'round
You know what to do
Come on people
Oh my land
What be troubling
Oh my land
What be troubling
What be troubling
What be troubling you

We are love and the future
We stand in the midst of fury and weariness
Who dreams of joy and radiance?
Who dreams of war and sacrifice?
Our sacred realms are being squeezed
Curtailing civil liberties
Recruit the dreams that sing for thee
Let freedom ring
Oh glad day

MOTHER ROSE

Mother rose
Every little morn'
To tend to me
There she stood
Waiting by the door
Selflessly
Took my hand
Took it with a smile tenderly
Mother rose
Every little morn'
To tend to me
Now's the time
To turn the view
Now that I have you

And I'll rise
Every little morn'
To tend to thee
When you rise
Open up your eyes
You will see
There I'll be
Waiting by the door
Come to me
Take my hand
Look into your heart
There I'll be
Now's the time
To turn the view
Now that I have you

Roses growing by my door
Climbing up the vine
All the thorns and pain obscured
Roses shall divine
Where we feel no pain
And the love inside
Where roses climb
Roses shall divine
Roses shall divine
Holy mother
Mother of gold
Mother with stories
Told and retold
She felt our tears
Heard our sighs
And turned to gold
Before our eyes
She rose into the light
She rose into the light
She rose into the light

—*for Beverly Williams Smith*

STRIDE OF THE MIND

I took a walk out to the sun
But I just, just couldn't take it
I followed a dream
It was circular
But I just, just could not fake it

Step to the left the left the left
Step to the right the right the right
Pick up the sign the sign the sign
For a stride of the mind the mind the mind

Simon of the desert
Blew into town
On the scalding tail
Of a bright cold wind
Slipped through the sand
Footprints emerged
Where no one was walking
Simon had been

Dropped from heaven
To a ready made world
Said I'm no Sufi
But I'll give it a whirl
We booked passage
On the Book of the Dead
Time to travel
Simon said

Step to the left the left the left
Step to the right the right the right
Pick up the sign the sign the sign
Oh the stride of the mind the mind the mind

Come on move where dreams increase
Where every man is a masterpiece
If you want to be counted
As another kind
And you're true, pursue
Stride of the mind the mind the mind
Stride of the mind the mind the mind

He bowed three times
Removed his fez
Pointed to heaven
And Simon says
The mind the mind the mind
Pick up the sign the mind the mind
It's a vertical climb the climb the climb
Stride of the mind the mind the mind
Pick up the sign the sign the sign
It's a vertical climb the climb
Take it in stride

CARTWHEELS

Come my one
look at the world
Bird beast butterfly
Girls sing notes of heaven
Birds lift them up to the sky

Spring is departing
Spring is departing

Your thoughts
Are darting like a rabbit
Like a rabbit cross the moon
Shining a light over your hair
As boys croon

Pretty in pink
It makes me wonder
What could ever
Bring you down
I see tears falling
From those eyes of brown

Hearing a voice,
You turn your head
You vanish, vanish
Into the mist
Of your thoughts

And I want to grasp
What brings you down

The world is changing
Your heart is growing

Open those eyes of brown

Hearing a voice
you turn your head
Girls turn by ones, by twos
Notes pour, glad and tender
To eradicate your blues

The good world, the good world
The good whirl, the good whirl

Come my one, look at the world
Bird beast butterfly
Girls sing notes from heaven
Birds lift them up to the sky

I see brown eyes
That see girls turning
Cartwheels cartwheels

I see brown eyes
I see a girl turning

Cartwheels, cartwheels

—for Jesse Paris Smith

PEACEABLE KINGDOM

Yesterday I saw you standing there
With your hand against the pane
Looking out the window at the rain
And I wanted to tell you
That your tears were not in vain
But I guess we both knew
We'd never be the same
Never be the same

Why must we hide all these feelings inside?
Lions and lambs shall abide
Maybe one day we'll be strong enough
To build it back again
Build the peaceable kingdom
Back again
Build it back again

Why must we hide all these feelings inside?
Lions and lambs shall abide
Maybe one day we'll be strong enough
To build it back again
Build the peaceable kingdom
Build it back again

—for Rachel Corey

GANDHI

I had a dream Mr. King
If you'll beg my pardon
I was trespassing
A sacred garden
And the blossoms fell
And they dropped like candy
And nature cried Gandhi Gandhi
And nature cried Gandhi Gandhi

When he was a boy
He was afraid of the dark
His mother would fast
And pray at his feet
And the lamp burned as he slept
Burned as he dreamed
He was dreaming of his sisters
Dressed in white muslin
Dancing in a ring
He was afraid of the dark
And the lamp burned
Dreaming of blossoms
They were burning his throat
He had eaten flowers
Flowers fell burning
From the young girls' hair
He was whispering
Into his god's ear
Let the children be so
And the lamplight flickered flickered
And his mother withered like Job

And he lay there dreaming
And the blossoms fell
And Tilak's trumpet
Proceeded to call
And the blossoms fell
And they dropped like candy
And the people cried Gandhi Gandhi

He was frail and shy
And the cast of his mind
Was mercurial
As the sacred verbs
Scrawled in the dust
On the floor, on the floor
Long live revolution
And the spinning wheel
And a handful of salt
The untouchables
Dropped like candy
They called to him Gandhi Gandhi
Feel our woes man of the giving
Rejoin the living Rejoin the living
Awake from the net
Where you've been sleeping
And climbing climbing
The flowing hair
And the golden flowers
Of the young girls
Awake little man
Awake from your slumber

And get 'em with the numbers
Get 'em with the numbers
One / Two / Three
Four hundred thousand million people
People / People / People
Awaken from your slumber

Long live revolution
And the spinning wheel
Awake awake
Is the mighty appeal
Oh, people awake
Awake from your slumber
And get 'em with the numbers
Get 'em with the numbers
I had a dream
Mr. King
If you'll beg my pardon
I was trespassing
The sacred garden
And the blossoms fell
Dropped like candy
And nature called Gandhi Gandhi
Gandhi Gandhi

Awake from your slumber
And get 'em with the numbers

Frankenstein

sitting

I loved my sister my gentle
innocent sister. when the
grief stricken father walked
senselessly with his dead child
in his hands, and Linda saying
will it be all night
I wanted to say yes

fling
ring
string
spring
bring
cling
RING   WING
SING

Our life is designed
with as a finishing line
that another sings
man small debts
as penned as regrets
upon a ragged wing

all life is
a manu designed
to leave us in Time
and bring may sing an me
on degradation

his life was designed
with a finishing line
that another shall sing.
and his small debts
penned as regrets —
upon a ragged wing

a life is designed
to depart in Time
wit us
and his small debts
penned as regrets
upon a ragged wing
I'm sorry my dear
that I won't be here
to take care of everything

he tells in his name
in sun and in rain

all life is designed
with a finishing line
that another say
and our small debts

Trespasses, 2004

TRESPASSES

Life is designed
With unfinished lines
That another sings
Each story unfolds
Like it was gold
Upon a ragged wing

The bold and the fair
Suffer their share
He whispered to his kin
All of my debts
Left with regrets
I'm sorry for everything

And she pinned back her hair
Shouldered with care
The burdens that were his
Mending the coat
That hung on the post
In heart remembering

Trespasses stretch
Like brown fences
Winding as they may
Trespasses stretch
Like broken fences
Hope to mend them one day

And her time was to come
Called to her son
This your song to sing
All of our debts
Wove with regrets
Upon a golden string

And he found the old coat
Hung on a post
Like a ragged wing
And took as his own
The sewn and unsown
Joyfully whistling

Trespasses stretch
Like broken fences
Winding as they may
Trespasses stretch
Like broken fences
Hope to mend them one day

IN MY BLAKEAN YEAR

In my Blakean year
I was so disposed
Toward a mission yet unclear
Advancing pole by pole

Fortune breathed into my ear
Mouthed a simple ode
One road is paved in gold
One road is just a road

In my Blakean year
Such a woeful schism
The pain of our existence
Was not as I envisioned

Boots that trudged
From track to track
Worn down to the sole
One road was paved in gold
One road was just a road

In my Blakean year
Temptation but a hiss
Just a shallow spear
Robed in cowardice

Brace yourself
For bitter flack
For a life sublime
A labyrinth of riches
Never shall unwind

The threads that bind
The pilgrim's sack
Are stitched
Into the Blakean back

So throw off your stupid cloak
Embrace all that you fear
For joy shall conquer all despair
In my Blakean year
In my Blakean year
In my Blakean year

BLAKEAN YEAR

In my Blakean year
I was so disposed
On a mission yet unclear
Advancing stroke by stroke
(as a timepiece never heard)

The labyrinth evolved
Always ~~unkened~~ at one end
Yet shackled round the bend
And all the wealth yielded
unrevealed

The laughter to digest
Beheld in mortal light
Just a test as God's jest
So throw down
Your stupid cloak
~~Adrift stroke by stroke~~
As a timepiece never heard
To be left less than dead

Yet joy stifled all despair
In my Blakean year

In my Blakean year
With a heavy load
One road was paved with gold
One road was just a road
~~The sun was like a silver spoon~~
~~And from the mouth it glowed~~
~~As the cock it crowed~~
~~Confronting~~ all that we hold dear
So throw down your stupid cloak
It's my Blakean year

confronting

awry

bone love

pawn
in
the
game
rythym
rythym

bone love eyes untired
feels like Truth denighed
you'll never be satisfied.
can The angels ring in jem
the bell within your brain !
an you more right with
the grain
not being with yourself.

Seduced .
so Seductive as one end
yet one
yet g shackled round The bend

walking the fire
walk The flood

Twist away in fear
of walk the
g good name is
as its sinking in The mud
as I walk The fire
ride The flood
water The.

as its sinking on the mud
of walk so

In My Blakean Year

CASH

Here we go around again
Curve of life spiraling
Everything we've ever known
As the seed of life gets blown
And the miracle of time
When will that time just end
Remember, you decide
Take that vow
Grab that ring
It's not a whim
Not a whim
When you be cashing in

Try to turn your life around
And all the things you do resound
And then you can't loose control
Say your time has come and then
Hard to pinpoint find the seam
Where that one time ends
Where that time begins
Remember, you decide
Take that vow
Take a stand
Grab that ring
It's not a whim
It's not a whim
It's only time
That you're cashing in

In the white noise of desire
We can't hear a single thing
Floating 'round the fragile bough
Afflictions of the human soul
Its beauty immaterial

You decide
Stand among the fallen ones
Take revenge defeated sons
Rend that coat
From seam to seam
It's only time
It's only time
That you spend
You spend
It's only life
That you're cashing in

RADIO BAGHDAD

Suffer not
Your neighbor's affliction
Suffer not
Your neighbor's paralysis
But extend your hand
Extend your hand
Lest you vanish in the city
And be but a trace
Just a vanished ghost
And your legacy
All the things you knew
Science, mathematics, thought
Severely weakened
Like irrigation systems
In the tired veins forming
The Tigris and Euphrates
In the realm of peace
All the world revolved
All the world revolved
Around a perfect circle
City of Baghdad
City of scholars
Empirical humble
Center of the world
City in ashes
City of Baghdad
City of Baghdad
Abrasive aloof

Oh, in Mesopotamia
Aloofness ran deep
Deep in the veins of the great rivers
That form the base of Eden
And the tree of knowledge
Held up its arms to the sky
All the branches of knowledge
All the branches of knowledge
Cradling Civilization
In the realm of peace
All the world revolved
Around a perfect circle
Oh Baghdad
Center of the world
City of ashes
With its great mosques
Erupting from the mouth of god
Rising from the ashes like a speckled bird
Splayed against the mosaic sky

We created the zero
But we mean nothing to you
You would believe
That we are just some mystical tale
We are just a swollen belly
That gave birth to Sinbad, Scheherazade
We gave birth to the zero
The perfect number
We invented the zero
And we mean nothing to you
Our children run through the streets

And you sent your flames
Your shooting stars
Shock and awe
Shock and awe
Like some, some
Imagined warrior production
Twenty-first century
No chivalry involved
No Bushido

Oh, the code of the West
Long gone never been
Where does it lie?
You came, you came
Through the west
Annihilated a people
And you come to us
But we are older than you
You wanna come
And rob the cradle
Of civilization
And you read Genesis
You read of the tree
You read of the tree
Beget by god
That raised its branches into the sky
Every branch of knowledge
In the cradle of civilization
Of the banks of the Tigris
And the Euphrates
Oh, in Mesopotamia

Aloofness ran deep
The face of Eve turning
What sky did she see
What garden beneath her feet
The one you drill
Pulling the blood of the earth
Little droplets of oil for bracelets
Little jewels sapphires
You make bracelets
'Round your own world
We are weeping tears rubies
We offer them to you
We are just
Your Arabian nightmare
We invented the zero
But we mean nothing to you
Your Arabian nightmare

City of stars
City of scholarship
Science
City of ideas
City of light
City of ashes
That the great Caliph
Walked through
His naked feet formed a circle
And they built a city
A perfect city of Baghdad
In the realm of peace
And all the world revolved

And they mean nothing to you
Nothing to you
Nothing

Go to sleep my child
Go to sleep
And I'll sing you a lullaby
A lullaby for our city
A lullaby of Baghdad
Go to sleep
Sleep my child
Sleep sleep sleep
Run run run

You sent your lights
Your bombs
You sent them down on our city
Shock and awe
Like some crazy t.v. show
They're robbing the cradle of civilization
They're robbing the cradle of civilization
They're robbing the cradle of civilization

Suffer not the paralysis of your neighbor
Suffer not but extend your hand

BANGA

Believe or Explode

AMERIGO

We were going to see the world
In this land we placed baptismal fonts
And an infinite number were baptized
And they called us Caribe
Which means men of great wisdom

Where are you going?
And are you going anywhere?
Where are we going?
Send me a letter
If you go at all

Ah the salvation of souls
But wisdom we had not
For these people had neither king nor lord
And bowed to no one
For they have lived in their own liberty

Where are you going?
And are you going anywhere?
Going in circles, going in circles anywhere
I saw and knew the inconstant shifting of fortune
And now I write to you
Words that have not been written
Words from the New World

Tracing the circles
Moving across my eyes
Lying on the ship
And gazing at the western sky
Tracing lazy circles in the sky

Hey—wake up!—wake up!

Where are you going?
And are you going anywhere?
Where are you going?
Send me a letter
If you go at all

It's such a delight to watch them dance
Free of sacrifice and romance
Free of all the things that we hold dear
Is that clear Your Excellency?
And I guess it's time to go but
I gotta send you just a few more lines
From the New World

Tracing the circles
Moving across my eyes
Lying on the ship
And gazing at the western sky
Tracing lazy circles in the sky

And the sky opened
And we laid down our armor
And we danced naked as they
Baptized in the rain
Of the New World.

APRIL FOOL

Come   be my April Fool
Come   you're the only one
Come   on your rusted bike
Come   we'll break all the rules

We'll ride like writers ride
Neither rich nor broke
We'll race through alleyways
In our tattered cloaks so

Come be my April Fool
Come we'll break all the rules

We'll burn all of our poems
Add to God's debris
We'll pray to all of our saints
Icons of mystery
We'll tramp through the mire
When our souls feel dead
With laughter we'll inspire
Then back to life again

Come   you're the only one
Come   be my April Fool
Come   Come
Be my April Fool
We'll break all the rules

FUJI-SAN

Oh mountain of our eyes
What do you see?
The girl with the almond eyes
Bowing to thee
Immortal soldiers
Clear the path
Shake the almond tree
Oh mountain of our eyes
Oh hear our plea
Oh hear our plea

See the five finger lakes
Like a hand in blue
Climbing sideways up the pure
To get a glimpse of you
To get a glimpse of you

The great lake
The white shirt
Your white cloak
Divine divine
Oh mountain
Of mine
Oh Fuji-San
We're climbing
Into the blue
Into the mist
Into the bright
Into your light

Oh mountain of our eyes
We're calling you
Will you hear our cries?
What will a poor boy do?
What will a poor girl do?

Hey!
We're calling to you
Oh Fuji-San
Oh Fuji-San
Oh Fuji-San

Oh mountain of our eyes
What do you see?
The girl with the almond eyes
Shaking her tree
Shake the almond tree

This is the girl for whom all tears fall
This is the girl who was having a ball
Just a dark smear masking the eyes
Spirited away buried in sighs.

This is the girl who crossed the line
This is the song of the smothering vine
Twisted a laurel to crown her head
Laid as a wreath upon her bed.

This is the blood that turned into wine
This is the wine of the house it is said
This is the girl who yearned to be heard
So much for cradling a smothering bird
This is the girl. This is the girl.

This is the girl for whom all tears fall
This is the girl who was having a ball
This is the laurel to crown her head
This is the wine of the house it is said.

This is the blood that turned into wine
This is the wine of the house it is said
This is the girl who cried to be heard
So much for cradling a smothering bird
This is the girl. This is the girl.

—*for Amy Winehouse*

TARKOVSKY

The eternal sun runs to the mother
She smoothes his brow and bids him
Drink from her well of hammered mist
Come along sweet lad, fog rises from the ground
The falling soot is just the dust of a shivering gem
The black moon shines on a lake
White as a hand in the dark
She lifts the lamp to see his face
The silver ladle of his throat
The boy the beast and the butterfly

The sea is a morgue, the needle and the gun
These things float in blood that has no name
The telegraph poles are crosses on the line
Rusted pins not enough saviors to hang
She blesses the road the noose of vine
And waits beneath the triangle
Formed by Mercury, an evening star
The fifth planet, with its blistering core
And the soaring eagle above and to the west
The boy the beast and the butterfly

She walks across a bridge of magpies
Her hollow tongue fills the brightness
With water and in the wink of an eye
One planet with a glittering womb
One white crow one diamond head
Big as a world big as a world
Don't forget how I played with you
She cries, and kissed away your tears
The white mouth of the sun smiles
On his beautiful tongue the seed of flight

MOSAIC

Last night in Konya
A voice carried me
To the pulpit of the arrow
Did you hear it too?
The oracle was written
On a silver leaf
Last night I read the words
Did you read them too?

Precious heart, precious seed
Precious life conceived
In a ring of fire
In a sleep of peace
Nothing stops desire
For the human beat

Last night was a rapture
In the mosaic sky
Dropping shards of love
Dropping shards of love

Precious heart, precious seed
Precious life conceived
In a ring of fire
In a sleep of peace
Nothing stops desire
For the human beat

I hunger for the cooling flame
I hunger for the infinite game

Last night in Konya
A voice carried me
To the pulpit of the arrow
Did you hear it too?
The oracle was written
On a silver leaf
Last night I read the words
Did you read them too?

Devour me, ah, devour me

Oh precious life
Oh precious seed
Oh precious heart
That beats
In a ring of fire
In a sleep of peace
Nothing stops
The human beat
The human beat

MARIA

At the edge of the world
Where you were no one
Yet you were the girl
The only one
At the edge of the world
In the desert heat
One shivering star
Sweet indiscreet

I knew you
When we were young
I knew you
Now you're gone

In a little Narcissus pool
Drawn by its spell
We saw ourselves
Raw excitable

I knew you
When we were young
I knew you
Now you're gone

We didn't know
The precariousness of our young powers
All the emptiness

Wild wild hair
Sad sad eyes
White shirt / black tie
You were mine

You grabbed the ring
Of the carousel
Tangoing
From Heaven
To Hell
I knew you

—for Maria Schneider

NINE

Night a nine of diamonds
A woman lay and cries
At the Sister of Mercy
On the Sabbath day

Night a nine of diamonds
As revelers commence
To shiver as she bore
In a babe, a radiance

Brave in constant motion
Wherein perfection brews
Darkness as his brother
Mischief as his moon

Summoning beneath
With his gypsy moves
Yearning as the foal
Shy and beautiful

Every card he drew
Had a different face
Lingering and lost
Unholy holy ghosts

I tend to play them all
He spoke with confidence
Another kind of strange
To shift in loneliness

He sought not for himself
The empire he would find
Save the golden womb
He enters in his mind

We will die a little
The rogues whistling
Nine blue-eyed sailors
Tip their caps to him

As he passes through them
More vagabond than king
With diamonds on his sleeves
Like a harlequin

—for John Christopher Depp

THE WING CHILD

O chariot of insect
O crown of wind
Two royal leopards
Run with him

On a golden lead
Of tapered vine
O the blood sky
O the blood sky

Wine of a God
Coupling wild
O golden seed
Who made the
Winged child

SENECA

Run, run my little one
Run out to sea
Run, run my little one
What do you seek?

The canvas is high
The scheme of a life
Written in the wind
The pen, the knife

Run, run my little one
Breathe a hymn to Him
Breathe my little one
The master is calling

If you were his eyes
If you were his dreams
The whole of the sky
Could not contain you

So run, run out to sea
Run, run my little one
Breathe a hymn
For Him
For thee

—for Seneca Sebring

BANGA

Loyalty rests in the heart of a dog
Don't sell all your eggs on the back of a frog
You can lick it twice but it won't lick you
And salivating salvation long so long so

Loyalty lives and we don't know why
And the paw is pressed against the nerve of the sky
You can leave him behind but he won't leave you
And the road to Heaven is true—true blue

Banga / Say—Banga

Loyalty lives and we don't know why
And his paws are pressed to the spine of the sky
You can leave him twice, but he won't leave you
And the way to Heaven is true—true blue

Banga / Say—Banga

Loneliness lifts when you open the night
Pilate awaits, as Jesus Christ
Forget him not—won't forget about you
The way to Heaven is blue—boo hoo

Banga / Say—Banga

Loyalty shifts if you carry a load
Ah, don't shit it out in a golden commode
You can kick him twice—it'll erode
Night is a mongrel—believe or explode

CONSTANTINE'S DREAM

In Arezzo I dreamed a dream
Of St. Francis who kneeled and prayed
For the birds and the beasts and all humankind

All through the night I felt drawn in by him
And I heard him call
Like a distant hymn

I retreated from the silence of my room
Stepping down the ancient stones washed with dawn
And entered the basilica that bore his name
Seeing his effigy I bowed my head
And my racing heart I gave to him
I kneeled and prayed
And the sleep that I could not find in the night
I found through him
I saw before me the world of his world
The bright field, the birds in abundance,
All of nature of which he sang
Singing of him
All the beauty that surrounded him as he walked
His nature that was nature itself
And I heard him—I heard him speak
And the birds sang sweetly
And the wolves licked his feet.

But I could not give myself to him.
I felt another call from the basilica itself
The call of art—the call of man
And the beauty of the material drew me away.

And I awoke, and beheld upon the wall
The dream of Constantine
The handiwork of Piero della Francesca
Who had stood where I stood
And with his brush stroked the legend of the True Cross
He envisioned Constantine advancing to greet the enemy
But as he was passing the river
An unaccustomed fear gripped his bowels
An anticipation so overwhelming that it manifested in waves.

All thru the night a dream drew toward him
As an advancing Crusade
He slept in his tent on the battlefield
While his men stood guard.
And an angel awoke him
Constantine within his dream awoke
And his men saw a light pass over the face of the King
The troubled King
And the angel came and showed to him
The sign of the true cross in heaven.
And upon it was written

In this sign shall thou conquer

In the distance the tents of his army were lit by moonlight
But another kind of radiance lit the face of Constantine
And in the morning light
The artist, seeing his work was done,
Saw it was good.

In this sign shall thou conquer

He let his brush drop and passed into a sleep of his own.
And he dreamed of Constantine carrying into battle in his right hand
An immaculate, undefiled single white Cross.
Piero della Francesca, as his brush stroked the wall
Was filled with a torpor
And fell into a dream of his own.

From the geometry of his heart he mapped it out
He saw the King rise, fitted with armor
Set upon a white horse
An immaculate cross in his right hand.
He advanced toward the enemy
And the symmetry, the perfection of his mathematics
Caused the scattering of the enemy
Agitated, broken, they fled.

And Piero della Francesa waking, cried out
All is art—all is future!
Oh Lord let me die on the back of adventure
With a brush and an eye full of light
But as he advanced in age
The light was shorn from his eyes
And blinded, he laid upon his bed
On an October morning in 1492, and whispered
Oh Lord let me die on the back of adventure
Oh Lord let me die on the back of adventure

And a world away—a world away
On three great ships
Adventure itself as if to answer
Pulling into the New World
And as far as his eyes could see
No longer blind
All of nature unspoiled—beautiful—beautiful
And such a manner that would have lifted
The heart of St. Francis
Into the realm of universal love

Columbus stepped foot on the New World
And witnessed beauty unspoiled
All the delights given by God
As if Eden had opened her heart to him
And opened her dress
And all of her fruit gave to him
And Columbus so overwhelmed
Fell into a sleep of his own
All the world filled his sleep
All of the beauty entwined with the future

The twenty-first century
Advancing like the angel that had come
To Constantine
Constantine in his dream
Oh this is your cross to bear
Oh Lord Oh Lord let me deliver
Hallowed adventure to all mankind

In the future
Oh art cried the painter
Oh art—Oh art—cried the angel
Art the great material gift of man
Art that hath denied
The humble pleas of St. Francis

Oh thou Artist
All shall crumble
Into dust
Oh thou navigator
The terrible end of man
This is your gift to mankind
This is your cross to bear
And Columbus
Saw all of nature aflame
The apocalyptic night
And the dream
Of the troubled King
Dissolved into light.

FUTURE AND FILM

Notes to the Future

What did we want
What did we ever want
To shake the fragile hands of time
To rip from their sockets
Deceiving eyes
To ride through the night
In a three cornered hat
Against the shadows
To cry Awake Awake
Wake up arms delicate feet
We are paramount then obsolete
Wake up throat wake up limbs
Our mantle pressed
from palm to palm
Wake up hearts dressed in rags
Costly garments fall away
Dangle now in truthful threads
That bind the breast
And wind the muscle
Of the soul and whole together

Listen my children and you shall hear
The sound of your own steps
The sound of your hereafter
Memory awaits and turns to greet you
Draping its banner across your wrists
Wake up arms delicate feet
For as one to march the streets
Each alone each part of another
Your steps shall ring
Shall raise the cloud
And they that will hear will hear
Voice of the one and the one and the one
As it has never been uttered before
For something greater yet to come
Than the hour of the prophets
In their great cities
For the people of Ninevah
Fell to their knees
Heeding the cry of Jonah
United covering themselves in sackcloth
And ashes and called to their God
And all their hearts were as one heart
And all their voices were as one voice
God heard them and his mind was moved
Yet something greater will come to pass
And who will call and what will they call
Will they call to God the air the fowl
It will not matter if the call is true
They shall call and this is known
One voice and each another
Shall enter the dead
The living flower
Enter forms that we know not
To be felt by sea by air by earth
And shall be an elemental pledge
This our birthright
This our charge
We have given over to others
And they have not done well
And the forests mourn the leaves fall
Swaddling babes watch and wonder
As the fathers of our spirit nations
Dance in the streets in celebration

As the mountains turn pale
From their nuclear hand
And they have not done well
Now my children
You must overturn the tables
Deliver the future from material rule
For the only rule to be considered
Is the eleventh commandment
To love one another
And this is our covenant
Across your wrist
This offering is yours
To adore adorn
To bury to burn
Upon a mound
To hail
To set away
It is merely a cloth merely our colors
Invested with the blood of a people
All their hopes and dreams
It has its excellence yet it is nothing
It shall not be a tyranny above us
Nor should God nor love nor nature
Yet we hold as our pleasure
This tender honor
That we acknowledge the individual
And the common ground formed
And if our cloth be raised and lowered
Half mast what does this tell us
An individual has passed
Saluted and mourned by his countrymen
This ritual extends to us all
For we are all the individual
No unknown no insignificant one
Nor insignificant labor nor act of charity
Each has a story to be told and retold
Which shall be as a glowing thread
In the fabric of man
And the children shall march
And bring the colors forward
Investing within them
The redeeming blood
Of their revolutionary hearts

Wim Wenders Film

no equation to explain the division of the senses

no sound to reflect the radiance of time

hands press against the sky, the soul foams

and light shoots from the face of the predator

in the beginning is dream

the milky corridor that shakes us out

and sends us reeling from site to site

forests and junkyards, halls of disorder

where we are swept to encircle dawn

strapped in a low car

racing thru silence

trumpeting bliss

you could kiss the world goodbye

or wake up

and kiss the world.

(Refrain)
can you feel
in the night
the world turn
round and round
wander wander
by the light
turning turning
in your eyes.

wander wander
guided by
endless eyes
~~endless light~~

Turning light

It Takes Time

IT TAKES TIME

No equation to explain the division of the senses
No sound to reflect the radiance of time
In the beginning is dream halls of disorder
Where we are swept to encircle dawn
Strapped in a low car racing
Thru silence trumpeting bliss
You could kiss the world goodbye

Standing outside the courthouse in the rain
Seemed like a lost soul from the chapel of dreams
With a handful of images
Faces of children phases of the moon
One little thing you get wrong changes
The dimensions streets, swept memory
Diffused and lost like a prayer in the sun

Sometimes you can't tell
Whether you're waking up or going to sleep
Spiraling unnumbered streets
All the games cannot be yours
All the sights, the treasures of the eye
Does the divided soul remain the same?
No equation to explain
Destiny's hand moved, by love
Drawn by the whispering shadows
Into the mathematics of our desire

—*for Wim Wenders's film* To the End of the World

MERMAID SONG

Do you remember me

The ocean rolled
Time was slow
We felt an energy
The cock was crowing
The rum was flowing

A mermaid burns to see
Beyond the sea
And if I could
Turn where you stood
Would you feel me
Would it be good
Would you remember

So turn the little key
The ocean rolls
Time is slow
Turn the little key
The cock is crowing
The rum is flowing

A mermaid burns to see
Beyond the sea
I long to see
I long to see
If there's a page for me

Do you remember me
The ocean rolled
Time was slow
We felt an energy
The cock was crowing
The rum was flowing

A mermaid burns to see
Beyond the sea
I long to see
I long to see
If there is a page for me
A page for me
In your diary.

—for the film Rum Diary

CAPITOL LETTER

Rebellion is a heart
breaking as the dawn
bursting into song
bursting into song

A bird in the hand
another role to play
mocking as the jay
mocking as the jay

She's the silent one
in her soft boots
racing thru the flames
racing thru the flames

She's the silent one
in her soft boots
drawing her bow
and her only truth

Rebellion is an arrow
wired to the sun
igniting everyone
igniting everyone

A bird in the hand
another role to play
mocking as the jay
mocking as the jay

She's the silent one
in her soft boots
drawing her bow
and her only truth

Racing thru the flames
in her soft boots
mocking as the jay
and she be mocking you

—*for the film* Hunger Games: Catching Fire

Wake up
Come—take my hand

Truth was like a dictionary
Urgent and sublime
We shook ourselves
Into the light
Like washing on a line
Like a gleaming sari
In the Indian wind
Wrapped in one another
Where pure hearts are kin

We ventured to the city
To the Chelsea Hotel
A place to lay our heads
A bit of heaven in hell
Entered the halls
Of our new university
They gave all the keys to you
And you offered them to me

In the blue night
You were bluer still
Your ankles tattooed with stars

We were so hungry
We could not sleep
And another hunger ensued
And we called out to Morpheus
To spread his cloak
On the world of our ways

You walked without fear
Toward the golden ladder
And I watched you
Climb rung by rung
Toward another kind of sun
And I went for another cup
It ran all over my dress
And you drank it up

Life to life
Scene to scene
Fortune's strife
Dream upon dream

Love was love
Art was art
Comingling in the heart
Kids
Just kids

MERCY IS

Mercy is as mercy does
Wandering the wild
The stars are eyes watching you
A breath upon a cloud

Two white doves
Two white wings
To carry you away
To a land in memory
A land in memory

The sky is high
The earth is green
And cool below your feet
So swiftly now
Beneath the bough
Your father waits for thee
To wrap you in
His healing arms
As the night sky weeps

For mercy is the healing wind
That whispers as you sleep

That whispers you to sleep.

—*for the film* Noah

poor fellah
for john walker lindh

an american /with a vision/of a religion/pure in it's
extent/studied at the madrasah in a remote corner/of
pakistan/tall bearded/almost a man/a model student
seeking the devout muslim life/an absolute
system/mathematically pure/on the northwest frontier no
longer alone/slept on a bed/of indian rope/full of
hope/poor dope/the heat and dust of april/drove him
away/into the cooler mountains/still seeking islam's
fountain/seven months premature/poor fellah /and easter
and passover/passed over/he journeyed to afghanistan/in
search of the pure /he gave them everything/he gave
them his heart he was so sure/poor fellah/walker was a
young man/embracing islam/walking with the
taliban/they captured his heart/he went through the
fazes/learning all the phrases memorizing pages/of the
koran/emerging on a saturday/ through a ruined avenue
crept from the underground/pine trees and debris/abdul
hamid/six nights in darkness without his catholic
father/and buddhist mother/separating treason and
dissent 16 to be a koranic scholar/19 to yemen to learn
arabic/went to afghanistan/to search for cooler
climates/to study the koran/pale as the sky/it attracted
his heart/if you be american/exercising freedom/looking
for something so pure/you may have to go and do
somethings/that other men/would not endure/he went to
the training camps/joined his brothers in kashmir/walked
a thousand miles/with the taliban/taken prisoner/during
the siege of kunduz/and marched to the fort/of certain
death/on the muddy outskirts/of mazar-i-sharif/ his
brothers died in ditches/in the open courtyards/their
faces blown/no one knew what the fuck was going on/who
was the enemy and who was the friend/and he wept/for
their corpses/that lay beneath the willows/walker was a
young man/walking with the taliban/embracing islam/it
attracted his heart/have a heart/have a heart/if you be a
christian/ exercise your wisdom/ forgive him/ have a
heart/ have a heart/ a heart

QANA

There's no one
In the village
Not a human
Nor a stone
There's no one
In the village
Children are gone
And a mother rocks
Herself to sleep
Let it come down
Let her weep

The dead lay in strange shapes

Some stay buried
Others crawl free
Baby didn't make it
Screaming debris
And a mother rocks
Herself to sleep
Let it come down
Let her weep

The dead lay in strange shapes

Limp little dolls
Caked in mud
Small, small hands
Found in the road
They're talking about
War aims

What a phrase
Bombs that fall
American made
The new middle east
The rice woman squeaks

The dead lay in strange shapes

Little bodies
Little bodies
Tied head and feet
Wrapped in plastic
Laid out in the street
The new middle east
The rice woman squeaks

The dead lay in strange shapes

Water to wine
Wine to blood
Ahh qana
The miracle
Is love

WITHOUT CHAINS

Five long years
was I a man
dreaming in chains
with the lights on
five long years
nothing to say
thoughts impure
at Guantanamo Bay

Now I'm learning
to walk without chains
I'm learning to walk
without chains
without chains

Born in Bremen
played guitar
a young apprentice
building ships
loved and married
heard the call
is attaining wisdom
a pursuit of fools?

Journeyed to Pakistan
to study Koran
taken in custody
no reason why
then a prison camp
no freedom to breathe

branded an enemy
an enemy

No fault was found
yet do they believe
then flown home
a version of free
chained to the floor
muzzled and bound
a last humiliation
left to endure

They say I walk strange
well that may be so
it's been a long time
since I walked at all

Now I'm learning to walk
without chains
to talk without chains
to breathe without chains
to pray without chains
to live without chains
to love without chains
without chains

—*for Murat Kunaz*

CHILD 13

Child 13 his father gone
Saw Jupiter ride
All the things
His father had known
Abided within him
Charity boy charity boy
You live you give
You groan you've grown
My heart's a stone
Your heart's a throne

Child 13 dreamed
He and his father did ride
The beaten track
The unbeaten track
The uncharted sky
His radiant face
Felt his father's eyes cry
Clarity boy, charity boy
You live, you give
You groan, you've grown
My heart's a stone
Your heart's a throne

In your hand a wand
A pen to pen
The physician within

I held you in my arms
I held you in my arms
I cradled you in my arms

BURNING ROSES

Father I am burning roses
father only God shall know
what the secret heart discloses
the ancient dances with the doe

Father I have sorely wounded
father I shall wound no more
I have waltzed among the thorns
where roses burn upon the floor

Daughter may you turn in laughter
a candle dreams a candle draws
the heart that burns
shall burn thereafter
may you turn as roses fall

MARIGOLD

He had a face of long ago
driven and strange with sad, sad eyes
and a smile to raise paradise

She tended her flock upon a hill
watched him from a place above
obscured by light, blushing gold

The heart is its own, yet not as god plans
and ne'er will she know so fine a man

Providence speaks another tongue
he traced the path of star and sun
and caught the eyes of the beguiled one

Through field and flower the poor girl fled
she raised her face her bonnet slid
he traced the path of star and sun
signs that marked the beguiled one

Faith has a flair divining good
her bonnet swept where he stood
he smoothed it out with his healing hand
and made his way into the cold, cold wind

The heart is its own, yet not as god plans
and ne'er will she know so fine a man

THE PRIDE MOVES SLOWLY

I heard you crying in your sleep
and stood above your contour there
I saw the moon behind your ear
wrists as mine, my mother's hair

I saw you with your father's arms
and so possess his blades,
protruding like small wings
I thought I'd never see again

The lamp of his boyhood glows,
the pride moves slowly
as in a dream. Circling
the shade's lucent plain

Bequeathed with certain calm,
the outline of their forms
diffuse as memories stream
sown in sadness, sleep

A WOMAN'S STORY

She stepped out from the caravan
Draped in white by attendants round
And a black top hat veiled in lace
And read the faces she laid down
She sang in her sleep
A woman's story
Just a diviner shuffling time
An image of a girl in a wedding gown
And her king his mane a crown
And she sang in her sleep
A woman's story
And the faces divined
Were their own

She raced through the hall
Like a young gazelle
Climbing the twilight painted sky
He drew her with a silken prayer
Into the calmness of his lair
And a garland of rubies for her hair
They drank from a cup never known
And her soul and his soul were as one
And they lie in their bed as ordained
Wrapped in an emerald sea of dreams
And she lifted her pale limbs
To the sadness of horns
Sounding him

And he died in her bed
Like a swallow
Beating to go home
But he just gave up
And fell thru the sky
Like an arrow
Thru the night
Thru the infinite

And she sang in her sleep
A woman's story
And the faces divined
Were their own

And her golden eyes sought
An emptiness
The twilight painted sky
Ruled by him
And to her life's
Only bliss
She returned
Like a lioness

LAUGHARNE

It was the town of Laugharne
Behind a gate of stone
The Merlin ring
Another winding wall
Where the voices find
A triangle of vine
He limped into town
A three-legged dog

Struck by lines
Infusing the air
Mighty charms
Tossed carelessly
It's not the rock, the rock
It's not the dome, the dome
It's not the wall, the wall
It's just a wall that's all

It was a tad unnatural
And his kingdom came
Through the moaning trees
New Jerusalem
The lamb but a babe
Stood by Raphael
And the summer man
Bared his hairy soul

Through mythology
Through the mystic fire
The way of prophecy
Is not the grail, the grail
Is not the bow, the bow
Is not the wall, the wall
It's just a wall, that's all

Ah, but give me a whirl
Come from this and that
You drop in my heart
Just a linear tale
Clarity revealed
To a three-legged dog
In the town of Laugharne
The new Jerusalem
With its solemn pines
And the small small homes
And an energy
Uncontained contained

It's not the rock, the rock
It's not the grail, the grail
It's not the wall, the wall
It's just a wall, that's all

THE WRITER'S SONG

I laid my mat among the reeds
I could hear the freemen call
oh my life what does it matter
will the reed cease bending
will the leper turn

I had a horn I did not blow
I had a sake and another
I could hear the freemen
drunk with sky
what matter my cry
will the moon swell
will the flame shy

Banzai banzai
it is better to write then die

In the blue crater
set with straw
I could hear
the freemen call
the way is hard
the gate is narrow
what matter I say
with the new mown hay
my pillow

I had a sake and another

I did not care to own nor rove
I wrote my name upon the water
nothing but nothing above

Banzai banzai
it is better to write then die

A thousand prayers
and souvenirs
set away in earthenware
we draw the jars
from the shelves
drink our parting
from ourselves

So be we king
or be we bum
the reed still whistles
the heart still hums

```
the writers song

i placed my mat
among the reeds
i could hear the freeman
who were drunk cry out
what matter what i say
will the reed cease bending
will the leper turn

in the blue crator
set with yellow hay
i could hear the freemen
drunk with sky
what matter my cry
will the moon swell
will the flame shy

i had a saki
and another
bonsai
a thousand souvineers
and a thousand prayers
and be we kings
or be we slaves
the reed still whistles
the heart still raves
the hand still grasps
a cup of love
nothing but nothing
above

i had a saki
and another
it is better to write
then die
bonsai
some scrawl their name
on the face of the water
on vellum sheets
on heavens border
to breathe well
is all one can ask
and to perform a task
formed by no other
```

travel to its own
book and the scars
within him from
his journeys produced
a least one
worthy work.
a thieves journal

The Writer's Song

Acknowledgments

The lyrics in this book are the result of four decades of collaboration. With the exception of a handful of my own songs, all of the music has been written or cowritten by these musicians:

Lenny Kaye, Ivan Kral, Richard Sohl, Jay Dee Daugherty, Allen Lanier, Oliver Ray, Tom Verlaine, Bruce Springsteen, Fred Sonic Smith, Jesse Paris Smith, and Tony Shanahan.

My grateful appreciation to Gabriella Doob and Suet Chong.

Royal image, page vi: © Oliver Ray.

Horses cover image, page 29: © Robert Mapplethorpe Foundation, Inc. Used with permission.

Dalai Lama, page 172: courtesy of Tibet Image Bank.

Handwritten lyrics and prayer shawl image, page 244, reprinted from the author's personal archives.

Index to Lyrics